STUDIES ON
VOLTAIRE AND THE
EIGHTEENTH
CENTURY

CLXXV

FOUNDED BY
THEODORE BESTERMAN

STUDIES ON VOLTAIRE AND THE EIGHTEENTH CENTURY

edited by

HAYDN MASON

VOLUME CLXXV

ENGLISH SHOWALTER, JR.

Madame de Graffigny and Rousseau:
between the two Discours

THE VOLTAIRE FOUNDATION
at the TAYLOR INSTITUTION
OXFORD

1978

ISSN 0435-2866

ISBN 0 7294 0113 8

PRINTED IN ENGLAND
BY
CHENEY & SONS LTD BANBURY OXFORDSHIRE

Madame de Graffigny and Rousseau:
between the two Discours

by English Showalter, Jr.

CONTENTS

9

ACKNOWLEDGMENTS

This study is one of several that I have done, or plan to do, based on the Graffigny papers. Many people have helped and encouraged me in my work during the past few years, and I am grateful to all of them. I would like to express my particular thanks to those who have helped with this volume: Marjorie Wynne of the Beinecke Library, who helped find and identify Rousseau's draft of *Les Saturnales*; R. A. Leigh, who authenticated Rousseau's handwriting at the beginning and who provided valuable editorial advice on the completed study; Paul S. Barrows, who informed me of the Vienna manuscript of *Les Saturnales* and lent me his microfilm of it; Walter Gordon, dean of Camden College, Rutgers University, and the Rutgers University Research Council, who have provided indispensable support for my research during the past three years; my colleagues in the French department of the University of Toronto, especially Alan Dainard and David Smith, with whom I am working on a *Correspondance complète de mme de Graffigny* and who have generously shared their vast knowledge of eighteenth-century France with me; and H. T. Mason, editor of *Studies on Voltaire and the eighteenth century*, whose friendship and support of my work have been invaluable to me.

ABBREVIATIONS

Best.D   *Correspondance and related documents*, ed. Theodore Bester-man, in *The Complete works of Voltaire* (1968-), vols.85-135.

GP   Graffigny papers, Beinecke Rare Book and Manuscript Library, Yale University.

Leigh   *Correspondance complète de Jean Jacques Rousseau*, éd. R. A. Leigh (1965-).

Œuvres   Rousseau, *Œuvres complètes*, éd. B. Gagnebin, Marcel Raymond, 'Bibliothèque de la Pléiade' (1959-).

I

Introduction: history of the Graffigny papers

A hitherto unknown manuscript by Rousseau, of the beginning of a play called *Les Saturnales*, is part of a massive collection of letters, manuscripts, and miscellaneous materials concerning madame de Graffigny, now in the Beinecke Library of Yale University, where it is catalogued as the Graffigny papers.[1] The letters which make up the largest part of the collection contain a certain number of passages relevant to Rousseau, including a full account of the origins of *Les Saturnales* and several firsthand impressions of Rousseau as he appeared in Paris society in the period between the two discourses. In this volume, it has been my primary purpose to make these important texts and documents available; and, in the interests of completeness, I have included all the references to Rousseau that I could find, however fleeting. I have at the same time provided more than a simple annotation; rather, I have tried to provide a full and authoritative description of the relationship between Rousseau and mme de Graffigny (which was in fact far different from what has been claimed previously), and to examine the ways in which these new details require us to modify our views of Rousseau and his activities during this period. The themes and events to be considered were determined, then, by the documents; and the coverage is far from systematic. I have followed a basically chronological order in the beginning, citing mme de Graffigny's references as they occur, and exploring the questions raised or answered. At the end, I have summarized the implications, using Rousseau's *Confessions* as the focus. And finally, I have included the text of the completed *Saturnales* as an appendix. Before approaching the contents, however, it seems desirable to explain the sources of the documents and to trace their history down to the present.

Madame de Graffigny was born Françoise d'Happoncourt in Nancy on 11 February 1695. On 19 January 1712, she married François Huguet de Graffigny, thus becoming mme de Graffigny as she is known to posterity. Her early life is obscure, and little of it need

[1] the Graffigny papers are quoted by permission of the Yale University Library.

concern us here.[2] Her husband died in 1725, and both her parents by 1733; she had no surviving children, and no brothers or sisters, and was therefore virtually on her own. She attached herself to the court of the duc de Lorraine, which was then flourishing in Lunéville.

In the late seventeenth century, Lorraine had suffered the horrors of war, as Louis XIV annexed the duchy of Lorraine by force of arms. In 1697, however, the treaty of Ryswick restored the duchy to its hereditary ruler, Léopold, who had been in exile in Austria. To secure the peace, Léopold married Elisabeth-Charlotte d'Orléans, sister of the duc d'Orléans who would be regent of France from 1715 to 1723. Under Léopold's rule, Lorraine prospered and Lunéville became an important cultural centre. Léopold died in 1729. His successor, François III, was still young, and moreover much more occupied with arranging an alliance with Maria-Theresa, daughter of the emperor, than with governing the duchy of Lorraine. His mother, known as Madame, became regent, and the ducal court continued to flourish. Mme de Graffigny was a minor figure there, but enjoyed the protection of Madame, so that these were some of the happiest years of her life.

In early 1736, however, a new treaty was signed in Vienna, which spelled the end of independence for Lorraine, and as a result, for mme de Graffigny. The chief provisions of this complicated agreement were that Stanislas Leszczynski would relinquish his claim to the throne of Poland, and would rule as king in Lorraine; François III would be compensated for the loss of his duchy by his marriage to Maria-Theresa and by the new title of grand-duke of Tuscany as soon as the incumbent died; Madame would retire to Commercy, which was set up as a principality for the rest of her lifetime; upon the death of king Stanislas, who was Louis XV's father-in-law, Lorraine would be reunited with France. Madame departed from Lunéville on 7 March 1737, and mme de Graffigny had to find a new protector.

A year and a half later, on 11 September 1738, mme de Graffigny herself left Lunéville.[3] Her destination was ultimately Paris, where

---

[2] a generally reliable account of mme de Graffigny's life, including her ancestry, family, and some historical background, can be found in Georges Noël, *Une 'primitive' oubliée de l'école des 'cœurs sensibles': madame de Grafigny* (Paris 1913). See especially pp.1-74.

[3] in my *Voltaire et ses amis d'après la*

correspondance de mme de Graffigny (Studies on Voltaire, cxxxix: 1975), there is a fairly detailed account of mme de Graffigny's life from her departure from Lunéville to the end of 1739. In addition, a team of scholars at the University of Toronto, under the general direction of J. A. Dainard, and with my participation, she was to become a lady-in-waiting to the duchesse de Richelieu, who was a princess of the house of Lorraine and a friend from earlier years. Being almost penniless, mme de Graffigny had to rely on the generosity of friends to make her way there; indeed, she had moved out of her own house in April, and lived with the comtesse de Grandville for several months before leaving Lunéville. Her route took her to Commercy, where old friends from Madame's entourage welcomed her for several days; then to Demange-aux-Eaux, where the marquise de Stainville-Choiseul kept her an unwilling guest for about two months; then on to Cirey, where an eagerly awaited visit with Voltaire and the marquise Du Châtelet turned into a nightmare when mme de Graffigny was accused, unjustly, of sending out copies of the forbidden poem, *La Pucelle*;[4] and at last to Paris, where she arrived in mid-February 1739.

The episode at Cirey is well known to eighteenth-century scholars, thanks to a series of thirty-one letters mme de Graffigny wrote during her stay to a friend back in Lunéville, François-Antoine Devaux, known to everyone as 'Panpan'.[5] They had corresponded as early as 1733, but a regular correspondence began the day mme de Graffigny left Lunéville, and continued with few interruptions until mme de Graffigny's death in December 1758. The two friends sent each other a letter by almost every one of the thrice-weekly posts, and actually wrote at least a few lines almost every day.

Panpan was born in 1712, and was thus seventeen years younger than mme de Graffigny. He studied law at Pont-à-Mousson in the early 1730s, and their friendship seems to have begun around that time; scattered letters exchanged between them have survived from the years preceding 1738. They were not lovers, but some evidence suggests that each was confidant for the other in an unhappy love affair of some kind. In any case, mme de Graffigny confided in Panpan about her liaison with Léopold Desmarest, an officer in the Heudicourt regiment; this was a relationship of many years' duration, which

is preparing a complete edition of mme de Graffigny's letters. Work on the letters to the end of 1739 is virtually finished, but details of publication are still uncertain.

[4] my article 'Sensibility at Cirey: mme Du Châtelet, mme de Graffigny, and the *Voltairomanie*', *Studies* (1975), cxxxv.181-92, examines this episode in close detail.

[5] the Cirey letters are available in the *Correspondence and related documents*, ed. Theodore Besterman, in *The Complete works of Voltaire* (Oxford 1968-), volumes 85-135. This is the so-called 'definitive edition' cited hereafter as Best.D. There are some supplementary notes to the Cirey letters in *Voltaire et ses amis*, pp.47-61.

did not end until 1743. Panpan spent most of a long life in idleness, never married, never earned a living, and indeed hardly wrote anything except personal correspondence, although he professed to have a vocation as a man of letters. It is difficult to understand what bonds kept him and mme de Graffigny in such close relations through so long a separation; perhaps their early sharing of unhappiness, their habit of confiding in each other, mme de Graffigny's loneliness, and Panpan's idleness all contributed. Whatever the reasons, the correspondence begun in September 1738 eventually totalled thousands of letters.

Mme de Graffigny's life in Paris did not go as she had planned.[6] The duchesse de Richelieu died in August 1740, abruptly terminating that hope. For two more years, mme de Graffigny lived as companion to wealthy old women. In the meantime she had slowly made friends among a circle of writers, artists, and literary hangers-on, the most notable being the retired actress, mlle Quinault *la cadette*, and her protector, the comte de Caylus. Together they sponsored a sort of salon, where a varied group of men and women met every week, ate moderately well, drank a lot, and spoke with complete freedom. Under their tutelage, mme de Graffigny began to write, first, in 1745 and 1746, a couple of anonymous stories; then in 1747, a novel, *Les Lettres d'une Péruvienne*. It was an instant success, and made its author a minor celebrity. In 1750, her tear-jerking drama *Cénie* was put on at the Théâtre français. It was a still greater triumph, and made her temporarily the leading woman of letters in Europe. Like any writer, she began to accumulate notes for future works, drafts, and copies of works she completed but in most cases never published. The most numerous of these are a series of playlets she wrote for the imperial court at Vienna. By a complicated and unexpected sequence of events, the ex-duke of Lorraine François and his wife Maria-Theresa became emperor and empress in 1745. Mme de Graffigny had many contacts among their courtiers, and as soon as she began to write she sought and got a small pension to supply edifying works for the imperial children.

[6] Noël's *Une primitive* may be consulted on mme de Graffigny's years in Paris, but it should be complemented by my articles 'The beginnings of madame de Graffigny's literary career', in *Essays on the age of the Enlightenment in honor of Ira O. Wade*, ed. Jean Macary (Paris 1977), pp.293-304; and 'Madame de Graffigny and her salon', in *Studies in eighteenth-century culture*, ed. Ronald C. Rosbottom (Madison 1977), vi.377-91.

Once *Les Lettres d'une Péruvienne* and *Cénie* had established her reputation, the size of the pension was increased, and the demand for the plays increased accordingly. By 1758, mme de Graffigny's star had already faded somewhat. She had tried to repeat her theatrical success with *La Fille d'Aristide* in May 1758, and it was a lamentable failure. Her health had been poor for years, and it began to decline seriously. For much of the year, she could not write herself, but had to dictate to a secretary. She died on 12 December, her mind still alert. In her will, she left various small legacies, which could not be paid, since she was badly in debt, as usual. Her papers, however, were all bequeathed to her faithful correspondent, Panpan Devaux.

It had been understood that Panpan would edit the papers, which included manuscripts of some of her works and of a large number of the unpublished plays; letters to mme de Graffigny from Panpan and from many other people, some of them famous; some occasional verse; and of course the numerous letters of mme de Graffigny herself, which were already in Panpan's hands. Alas, Panpan had never been able to accomplish much on his own behalf, and he made no headway with mme de Graffigny's legacy, if indeed he tried. The text of *La Fille d'Aristide* had been prepared before she died, and it appeared in 1759; it did nothing to encourage further publications. In 1770 there appeared *Œuvres posthumes* of mme de Graffigny, which consisted of two short plays, *Ziman et Zenise* and *Azor*. It is not likely that Panpan had anything to do with them, for they had been produced long before on private stages, and copies were thus available elsewhere. And so the papers lay, pretty much undisturbed, except that the collection grew as Panpan added to it letters he received from various friends.

The subsequent fate of the papers has been told in part by mme de Graffigny's biographer, Georges Noël.[7] Panpan lived to see the Revolution, and died a bachelor in his native Lunéville on the 11th of April 1796. He bequeathed the papers then to an old friend, mme Durival, whose husband had held various offices under Stanislas and in the French ministry of foreign affairs, and who was at the time living in the village of Sommerviller near Lunéville. She was no better prepared than Panpan to edit such a mass of papers, and so on her

---

7 Noël, *Une primitive*, pp.x-xvi, 359-77.

death in 1819 they passed to her adopted children, Joseph-Louis-Gabriel Noël and his wife Charlotte-Suzanne-Adélaïde de Vismes d'Aubigny. In the interval, however, the chevalier de Boufflers, having returned from the emigration, asked to see the letters and did get at least some of them around 1806. Georges Noël, a descendant of this couple, relates a family legend that most of the papers were turned over to a Russian, count Orloff, who was presumably responsible for extracting the letters written from Cirey, and having them published in 1820 with the title *Vie privée de Voltaire et de mme Du Châtelet.* The relatively small number of papers remaining in the family's possession then served as the basis for Georges Noël's biography, *Une 'primitive oubliée' de l'école des 'cœurs sensibles': mme de Graffigny,* published in 1913. These 'Noël' papers included two letters written by mme de Graffigny right after the Cirey episode, but primarily letters to mme de Graffigny from Galli de Bibiena, Bret, père Martel, mme de Barbarat, Liébault, and others. There were also letters from Liébault to Devaux, that mme de Graffigny surely never saw at all, and others written to Devaux after mme de Graffigny's death. The leads Georges Noël had provided were never followed up, and after the first world war, the 'Noël' portion of the papers was for all practical purposes lost again. I have, however, made contact with his heirs, who have very graciously allowed me to examine the papers they still possess; some things quoted by Georges Noël remain unaccounted for, but the main sources for his biography have been located.

In 1965, the 'Orloff' portion reappeared, when it was auctioned by Sotheby.[8] It had ultimately been purchased by the great English bibliophile, sir Thomas Phillipps (1792-1872), who amassed a collection of incredible size in the early nineteenth century. Portions of it have been sold periodically since before 1900, and there are several volumes of catalogues of the papers purchased by the Bibliothèque nationale alone. Moreover, the collection is still being sold off. During the second world war, the books and manuscripts were hastily packed and stored for protection. Afterwards, the trustees concluded that the library could never be reconstituted as a private institution and

[8] Sotheby catalogue, *Bibliotheca Phillippica,* 1965, part 1, sale of 28 June 1965, pp.43-60, lots 114-132.

determined to sell all the collections. The Graffigny papers made up only a few lots in a two-day sale; the bulk of the collection, some seventy-eight volumes, was purchased by H. P. Kraus, who then donated all of it to Yale, except for the manuscripts of the letters from Cirey. The documents used in the present study derive from this group of papers, now available to scholars at the Beinecke rare book and manuscript library of Yale University. The collection includes the series of letters from mme de Graffigny to Devaux, from 1738 to 1758, complete except, as noted, for the Cirey letters, which are presumably still in mr Kraus's possession, and a few stray letters in other libraries. The other lots sold by Sotheby in 1965 are now in the Bibliothèque nationale; they include letters addressed to mme de Graffigny, several volumes of verse and fragments, and some other papers of no apparent relevance to mme de Graffigny.[9] In short, very nearly all of Devaux's original accumulation now seems to have been located. The texts cited in this volume all derive from the Graffigny papers at the Beinecke library; precise locations and the circumstances of their composition will be explained as they are presented.

9 Bibliothèque nationale, mss. N. a. fr.15579-15581, 15589-15592.

II

Mme de Graffigny and Jean-Jacques Rousseau

Everyone today would agree that, broadly speaking, mme de Graffigny's works contain pale foreshadowings of Rousseau's. *Les Lettres d'une Péruvienne* is, like *La Nouvelle Héloïse*, an epistolary novel; both combine a pathetic love story and social criticism – indeed, many specific subjects, such as the opera or education, come up for commentary in both books. In both, there is a simultaneous exaltation of passion and virtue, and mme de Graffigny clearly exploits the eighteenth-century taste for sentimentality. Although there is no evidence that Rousseau read *Les Lettres d'une Péruvienne*, he did praise *Cénie* in the *Lettre à d'Alembert*. In fact, a certain kinship of spirit was noticed at least as early as 1752, by the Swiss Isaak Iselin, who journeyed to Paris that year, met both writers, and noted in his journal that 'bien qu'elle déclame tant contre le bon Rousseau elle ne laisse pas d'exprimer des sentiments analogues aux siens dans ses *Lettres d'une jeune Péruvienne*'.[1] It would appear that the young Turgot, one of mme de Graffigny's inner circle of admirers, had observed the analogies the year before, when he wrote a long letter suggesting possible ways to expand and revise the novel. Even though Rousseau is never named, the first *Discours* is the likely target of these remarks: 'Que Zilia pèse encore les avantages réciproques du sauvage et de l'homme policé. Préférer les sauvages est une déclamation ridicule. Qu'elle la réfute . . .'[2]

At the same time, no one today would want to make very much of mme de Graffigny as an influence or even precursor; most of the parallels can be attributed to the fact that she and Rousseau were contemporaries, and thus interested in the same questions and dependent on the same sources of information. For the century and a half

---

[1] Isaak Iselin, *Pariser Tagebuch 1752*, ed. Ferdinand Schwarz (Basel 1919), p.167. A number of excerpts relating to Rousseau, including the one just cited, are reprinted in Jean-Jacques Rousseau, *Correspondance complète*, ed. R. A. Leigh (Oxford 1965-), appendix 83p. Subsequent references to this edition will be given in the text.

[2] Anne-Robert-Jacques Turgot, *Lettre à madame de Graffigny sur les Lettres Péruviennes* (1751), in *Œuvres*, ed. Eugène Daire (Paris 1844), ii.786. Turgot's letter is also available in mme de Graffigny, *Lettres d'une Péruvienne*, ed. Gianni Nicoletti (Bari 1967), pp.459-74.

after her death, mme de Graffigny was regarded as one very minor manifestation of a wave of new ideas that was sweeping across Europe at the time. In histories of literature large enough to mention her at all, she found her place naturally in chapters on 'sensibilité' or 'roman épistolaire' or 'comédie larmoyante', fashions which constituted the preparation of a public for Rousseau's brilliant and original use of the same themes and materials. When an occasional scholar took special notice of mme de Graffigny herself, it was in the same spirit; for example, Louis Etienne wrote in 'Un roman socialiste d'autrefois':

[Mme de Graffigny] a été la première de son temps, au moins dans la littérature proprement dite, à faire le procès du luxe; elle a précédé Rousseau sur ce point comme sur quelques autres. Il n'y a pas lieu d'en être surpris: elle venait d'une province éloignée, indépendante, sinon d'une république étrangère à la France; elle était pauvre comme lui; comme lui elle avait atteint, dépassé même le moment où un écrivain a toutes les idées personnelles qu'il aura, qu'il est capable d'en avoir; comme lui elle publiait, aux environs de cinquante ans, le livre où elle mettait tous les sentiments de son âme; le rapprochement de ces deux esprits si fort disproportionnés n'a pour but, on le sent, que de montrer leurs analogies.[3]

None of these comments, obviously, claims to show any influence of mme de Graffigny on Rousseau, much less direct personal contacts. Rousseau does mention mme de Graffigny twice, once as I have said in the *Lettre à d'Alembert*, where he mentions *Cénie* as a play where women are depicted in a deceptively idealized manner, and then comments in a footnote:

Ce n'est point par étourderie que je cite *Cénie* en cet endroit quoique cette charmante pièce soit l'ouvrage d'une femme: car, en cherchant la vérité de bonne foi, je ne sais point déguiser ce qui fait contre mon sentiment; et ce n'est pas à une femme, mais aux femmes que je refuse les talents des hommes. J'ignore d'autant plus volontiers ceux de l'auteur de *Cénie* en particulier qu'ayant à me plaindre de ses discours, je lui rends un hommage pur et désintéressé, comme tous les éloges sortis de ma plume.[4]

The incident referred to was responsible for the second allusion, in the *Confessions*, ix. Rousseau is relating the history of his quarrel with

[3] Louis Etienne, 'Un roman socialiste d'autrefois', *Revue des deux mondes* (15 juillet 1871), xciv.454-64; also reprinted in Graffigny, *Lettres d'une Péruvienne*, ed. Nicoletti, pp.478-92.

[4] Jean-Jacques Rousseau, *Lettre à m. d'Alembert sur les spectacles*, in *Œuvres complètes* (Paris 1852), iii.134n.

Diderot, who had just been accused of plagiarizing *Le Fils naturel* from Goldoni. Wrote Rousseau: 'Mad^e de Grafigny avoit même eu la méchanceté de faire courir le bruit que j'avois rompu avec lui à cette occasion.'[5] Certainly Rousseau's remark implies no real contacts between him and mme de Graffigny, and indeed, the actual source of the remark can be traced to a letter from Deleyre to Rousseau, dated 23 August 1757, in which he says, still on the subject of Diderot's troubles: 'Le déchainement est tous les jours plus terrible, Madame de Grafigny fait courir le bruit que vous avés rompu avec votre ami, depuis qu'on le traite si mal' (Leigh 518). Deleyre's letter was published in 1865, and seemed to explain fully the tenuous but only demonstrable link between them.

It was Georges Noël, in his biography of mme de Graffigny, not published until 1913, who proposed for the first time that there had been direct and even close personal contacts. The passage he devoted to Rousseau must be quoted in full, despite its length:

Rousseau avait évolué plus lentement et plus méthodiquement qu'il ne le dit vers le mépris ou mieux vers la haine de son siècle. Mme de Grafigny, qui, trois ans auparavant, avait exprimé sous les quipos de Zilia, et sans savoir leur donner le même éclat, des reproches pareils, eut-elle quelque influence sur lui? Cela n'est pas invraisemblable.

Il ne paraît pas douteux que vers ce temps-là, et depuis quelques années déjà, le 'Genevois' et la 'Grosse' aient fait échange de doléances sociales et commerce de misanthropie. Il pourrait donc fort bien se faire que Mme de Grafigny ait en une modeste part dans la fameuse évolution morale que subit alors le citoyen de Genève et qu'il raconte après l'avoir dramatisée.

On en retrouve la trace, en incidente, dans plus d'un document que j'ai sous les yeux. Et je puis bien avouer que la seule chose qui me fasse hésiter à le dire, c'est précisément la crainte de ce ridicule dans lequel on tombe si facilement, eu prétendant apercevoir partout l'influence d'un personnage modeste que l'on étudie.

Ce que les documents disent en tout cas, c'est que Rousseau était parfois prié presque tout seul à la modeste table de la bonne dame et qu'il y venait quand un accès de 'noir' ne le faisait pas 'fuir à la vue de ce plaisir.'*

Ce que les documents permettent encore d'affirmer, c'est que Mme de Grafigny et Rousseau, suivant la mode de leur temps, se plaisaient à des échanges de vues, par causerie ou par lettres, sur divers sujets de philosophie, de sentiment ou de religion.

Et le galant Bret recevait de sa vieille amie communication des lettres du 'Genevois' et lui écrivait: 'Je vous renvoie les lettres de ce grand Rousseau dont la dévotion m'a touché.'*

Ralph Leigh, in his *Correspondance complète de Jean Jacques Rousseau*, has already called attention to the unfortunate confusion here of Jean-Jacques with Jean-Baptiste Rousseau. The letters of the latter were published in Holland in 1750, and clearly it is to them that Bret refers (Leigh, app.81, notes, esp. *a*). Leigh does see in these lines 'une confirmation des rapports qui existaient à cette époque entre JJ, Bret et mme de Graffigny'. The brief reference to 'le Genevois', however, could well be only a stylistic flourish, appropriate because the first *Discours* had just been published in January 1751, which is no doubt the correct date for this letter. If Noël had had any more explicit documents, he would certainly have cited them; the 'plus d'un document' probably refers to the two letters here cited, and no more. Noël also inferred from Bret's use of the pet name 'maman' that they had picked that up from Rousseau, an argument too farfetched to require refutation. The truth is, in fact, that the documents quoted by Noël not only do not prove personal contacts between Rousseau and mme de Graffigny, but do not even refer to any such contacts. Noël's premises for all his inferences are totally false.

Literary history is not without irony, however, and false premises do not necessarily lead to false conclusions. Noël had hit on the truth in spite of everything, and confirmation was not long in coming. Just six years later, Ferdinand Schwarz edited and published Isaak Iselin's

---

* Bret à Mme de Grafigny, fin de 1750(?) acceptant à dîner chez son amie, tandis que Rousseau refuse par accès d'hypocondrie: 'J'aurai l'honneur d'aller chez vous avec ma gaieté, et vous ferez de moi tout ce qu'il vous plaira toute la journée. Grillez-moi; retenez-moi; enfermez-moi; je serai tout à vous: le Genevois a fui à la vue du plaisir . . .' [note of Noël].

Du même à la même et vers le même temps: 'Je vous renvoie la lettre singulière du Père Martel; elle est à garder. Son zèle et son amitié m'ont touché ainsi que la dévotion de ce grand Rousseau dont je vous renvoie les lettres. Adieu, maman. Mille baisers' [note of Noël].[6]

[6] Noël, *Une primitive*, pp.292-3.

Pariser Tagebuch 1752. Iselin was a young Swiss who took a trip to Paris in the spring of 1752. He had read and become deeply interested in Rousseau's *Discours* and the refutations it provoked. Through the intermediary of Grimm, he met Rousseau in Paris, and of course recorded parts of their discussions. In June 1752, he discussed Rousseau with mme de Graffigny, and his account of these conversations makes it clear that they knew each other. When Noël's book first appeared, little heed had been paid to the claims about Rousseau, although the war may have been more responsible for that than scholarly judgement. Still, it seems doubtful that Noël's evidence alone would have been persuasive; combined with Iselin's diary, it seemed very persuasive indeed.

As a result, it became part of the accepted knowledge about Rousseau that he had been a guest at mme de Graffigny's salon, perhaps even an intimate friend, in the late 1740s and early 1750s. A few, like Bruwaert, speculated on the mutual influences and made of the relationship a significant part of Rousseau's life.[7] But more cautious and conscientious scholars also relied on the fact as demonstrated; Courtois, in his 'Chronologie critique de la vie et des œuvres de Jean-Jacques Rousseau' proposed the salon of mme de Graffigny as the likeliest place for Voltaire to have seen Rousseau, as he claimed later to have done once only in his life.[8] This plausible hypothesis has been accepted by virtually all scholars since, with varying degrees of prudence. The Pléiade edition of the *Confessions*, for example, says: 'En 1750, les deux hommes se rencontreront vraisemblablement chez Mme de Graffigny' (*Œuvres*, i.1384). Let us begin, then, by examining this question in detail.

[7] Edmond Bruwaert, 'Madame de Graffigny et Jean-Jacques Rousseau', *Revue hebdomadaire* (1924), viii.567-92.

[8] Louis-J. Courtois, *Chronologie critique de la vie et des œuvres de Jean-Jacques Rousseau* (Annales Jean-Jaques Rousseau, xv.1923).

III

When did Voltaire meet Rousseau?

According to Voltaire himself, 'Je n'ai vu qu'une seule fois en ma vie le Sr Jean Jaques Rousseau à Paris, il y a vingt cinq ans' (Leigh 1975, Best.D10578). Most of the scholarly effort that has gone into this question has taken off from that sentence, penned in a letter to Charles Pictet of approximately 9 July 1762. By then, of course, Rousseau's break with the *philosophes* was complete, and Voltaire was bent on destroying Rousseau's reputation, if he could. This little comment contains nothing very damaging, to be sure, but its tone is clearly contemptuous and dismissive, suggesting the possibility of some exaggeration for greater rhetorical effect.

For it is quite impossible to take the twenty-five years as an exact figure; in 1737 neither Jean-Jacques nor Voltaire was in Paris, nor indeed at any date close to it. Consequently, attention has been focused on the infrequent epistolary contacts between the two men, in the hope of finding some trace of a personal contact.

The earliest exchange of letters took place in 1745, when Rousseau had been charged by the duc de Richelieu with writing music for *Les Fêtes de Ramire*, which was a reworking of Voltaire's *Princesse de Navarre*. On 11 December Rousseau wrote Voltaire a letter announcing the completion of some of the music, and begging his approval in a style of excessive humility such as one would expect from an unknown addressing a master. A few days later Voltaire responded with the self-assured generosity and flattery one would expect from a master addressing an unknown (Leigh, 139, 140; Best.D3269, D3270). From these two letters, one would imagine the 'collaboration' to have launched their relationship auspiciously; but the *Confessions* tell a different story: Rousseau's music was criticized for qualities owing to Voltaire's words; eventually the job was given back to Rameau, Rousseau's enemy. From the experience and his hard work, Rousseau got neither praise, nor reward, nor even simple recognition, at least as he remembered it.

Five years later, in 1750, the two men exchanged a second round of letters. This time, the pretext was a mysterious incident at the Théâtre français, where Voltaire's *Oreste* was playing to mixed responses.[1] It has long been supposed that what really happened was that Pierre Rousseau, of Toulouse, a minor writer and future editor of the *Journal encyclopédique*, had joined in heckling the play.[2] Voltaire had quarrelled with him in the theatre, whereupon Jean-Jacques Rousseau wrote to Voltaire to assure him that it was not Rousseau of Geneva who had attacked him. It happened that mme de Graffigny was in the theatre that evening, and her account makes it possible to confirm that version of the events.

After her visit to Cirey in 1738-1739, and her subsequent quarrels with mme Du Châtelet, mme de Graffigny had no personal contacts with Voltaire in the 1740s. In September 1749, however, mme Du Châtelet died, and Voltaire came to Paris. He made overtures of friendship to mme de Graffigny, and finally invited her and her niece, Minette de Ligniville, the future mme Helvétius, to attend a performance of *Oreste* on Wednesday, 28 January 1750, in the company of mme Denis, Voltaire's niece (Best.D4108, D4109). It was during this evening that the Rousseau incident took place; mme de Graffigny described it as follows:[3]

Je t'ai dit, je crois, que mercredi on vint dire a sa niece qu'il avait eu une querelle a l'enphitheatre. C'etoit avec Rousseau, l'auteur de la *Ruse inutile*.[4] Il etoit a cote de V[oltaire] et disoit ce qu'il pensoit de la piece, rioit meme quelquefois. V[oltaire] inpatianté demande a son autre voisin, 'Qu'est-ce que cet homme, n'est-ce pas un nommé Rousseau?' Celui-ci demande du meme ton a son autre voisin, 'Qu'e[s]t-ce que cet homme, n'est-ce pas un nommé V[oltaire]?' V[oltaire] lui dit qu'il est bien M[onsieu]r pour lui. L'autre lui repond les memes parolle. Voltaire replique et l'autre repond toujours parolle pour parolle. La scene dura quelque tems. Enfin V[oltaire] sort en colere et va deffendre au bureau des billets qu'on laisse jamais entrer Rousseau a ses piece. On lui rit au nez. Il va a l'exemp et lui dit d'arreter Rousseau, qu'il s'en charge aupres de Mr Berier.[5] L'exemp s'informe et

---

[1] on the background of *Oreste*, see Henry C. Lancaster, *French tragedy in the time of Voltaire* (Baltimore 1950), ch.13, pp.333-60; and Paul O. LeClerc, *Voltaire and Crébillon père: history of an enmity* (Studies on Voltaire, cxv: 1973).

[2] the chief source is Charles Collé, *Journal et mémoires*, ed. Honoré Bonhomme (Paris 1868), i.126.

[3] to Devaux, 1 February 1750 (GP, xlvi.146-7).

[4] Pierre Rousseau; the play was presented on 6 October 1749 and printed soon after; see Leigh 149.

[5] Nicolas Berryer (d. 1762), lieutenant-général of police.

refuse d'arreter. V[oltaire] en fureur s'en retourne sur le theatre, trouve le chevalier de Mouy,[6] le prend pour le plastron de sa fureur, lui chante pouille. On s'assemble. Mouy revolté prend l'assemblée a temoin de l'ingratitude de V[oltaire]. Il fait une courte recapitulation des servisses qu'il lui a rendu, et dit-il, 'Mesieurs, encore aujourd'huy j'ai courus tous le jour, et je lui ai ammené trois fiacrées des mieux choisies que j'ai pu.' Aux trois fiacrées toute l'assemblée eclate de rire et V[oltaire] s'enfuit. Cela n'est-il pas bien plaisant?

Rousseau wrote to Voltaire on 30 January 1750, denying any part in the incident, but surrounding his explanation with some rather ambiguous apologies.[7] Rousseau must have been working on his first *Discours* at about this time, and some of his revived republican fervour seems to have inspired him. This is the first known text which he signed 'Jean-Jaques Rousseau, citoyen de Genève'. Voltaire replied not long afterwards in a courteous but chilly note, accepting the essential factual point that Jean-Jacques was not the guilty party (Leigh 149, 150).

A final exchange occurred in 1755, when Rousseau sent Voltaire a copy of his second *Discours*. Voltaire, in exile near Geneva, and assailed by many troubles, seized the occasion to write a letter of thanks which was also a counter-attack on what he obviously perceived as his and Rousseau's common enemies. Voltaire treats Rousseau's ideas – and it is apparent that he is thinking primarily if not entirely of the first *Discours*, and may not even have read the second yet – with witty detachment, as if they were intellectual games and entertaining paradoxes. This is no doubt what Rousseau meant when he wrote in his *Confessions*, concerning the 1745 letter from Voltaire: 'Qu'on ne soit pas surpris de la grande politesse de cette lettre comparée aux autres lettres demi-cavalieres qu'il m'a écrites depuis ce tems-là' (*Œuvres*, i.336). In September 1755, however, Rousseau was willing to reply very much in the same spirit, in spite of his statement in the *Confessions*: 'La lettre que Voltaire écrivit sur mon dernier ouvrage me donna lieu d'insinuer mes craintes dans ma réponse; l'effet qu'elle produisit les confirma' (*Œuvres*, i.396). Rousseau's editors and commentators have been hard pressed to find anything resembling

---

[6] Charles de Fieux, chevalier de Mouhy, novelist, journalist, police spy; among other services to Voltaire, he had lent his name to *Le Préservatif*, the attack on Desfontaines (1738).

[7] in a separate article (forthcoming), I have studied the significance of Rousseau's letter.

insinuations of fears in this letter. These two important letters, both published soon afterwards in the *Mercure*, were followed by two notes in which Voltaire asked, and Rousseau granted, permission for the publication of Voltaire's letter.

Nothing in any of these letters suggests that the two writers were personally acquainted. Each of the three episodes involves the formal courtesies and employs the appropriate tone for two professional men of letters of the time. One can watch a progress in Rousseau's role, from the obscure hopeful of 1745 to the still unknown but recently inspired author of the first *Discours* in 1750 to the celebrity of 1755, author of two notorious discourses, a popular opera, a play, several polemical works, and numerous articles on music for the *Encyclopédie*. One can see also variations in Voltaire's status, from powerful dispenser of favours in 1745, to vexed and harassed failure in 1750, to combattant in 1755. As far as a meeting between the two men is concerned, however, one may conclude only this: since it must have occurred before 1755, it was so insignificant a moment that it had no effect whatsoever on their relationships.

In general, the incident in the theatre in January 1750 has come in for special scrutiny. Having only the letters to go on, scholars have uniformly assumed that Voltaire had falsely accused Jean-Jacques. Desnoiresterres, for example, wrote: 'Voltaire précisément alors, sur des rapports mensongers, se répandait en plaintes contre Jean-Jacques, et s'attirait de ce dernier une lettre digne, fière, mais polie et respectueuse, où le citoyen de Genève se défendait avec indignation de torts qu'il n'aurait jamais . . .'[8] The false reports that led Voltaire astray are, so far as I can tell, a pure hypothesis on Desnoiresterres's part; but later scholars accept that version without hesitation. Crocker, for example: 'Early in 1750, Rousseau had had a second exchange of letters with Voltaire, who had confused him with a dramatic writer, Pierre Rousseau, one of Voltaire's innumerable enemies';[9] or Guéhenno: 'Un soir qu'on jouait au Théâtre-Français une pièce de Voltaire, le parterre avait fait du bruit. Voltaire était là. Le meneur du bruit se nommait Rousseau, et Voltaire crut avoir affaire au 'petit Rousseau' qui jadis avait travaillé pour lui. Voici comment Jean-Jacques prévenu

[8] Gustave Desnoiresterres, *Voltaire et la société au XVIIIe siècle* (Paris 1871), iii.358.

[9] Lester G. Crocker, *Jean-Jacques Rousseau: the quest (1712-1758)* (New York 1968), p.216.

se disculpa . . .'[10] Thus some scholars reason that Voltaire must never have seen Jean-Jacques, or else he would not have made the mistake. In writing to apologize, Jean-Jacques does not remind Voltaire of any meeting, nor suggest that he ought to have recognized him. Therefore, it is argued, the meeting Voltaire remembered must have taken place some time after 30 January 1750.[11] Furthermore, since Voltaire himself went to Prussia in June 1750, and did not return to Paris until well after 1762, the meeting must have taken place between 30 January 1750 and June 1750, whether or not it was at mme de Graffigny's salon.

Very little of that reasoning is sound, however. It is, first of all, not certain – even with mme de Graffigny's testimony – exactly what Voltaire was thinking when he accosted Pierre Rousseau in the theatre. Mme de Graffigny – and her account has some support from other sources[12] – reports that Voltaire said, 'Qu'est-ce que cet homme, n'est-ce pas un nommé Rousseau?' Now if we suppose that Voltaire meant by this 'le nommé Jean-Jacques Rousseau', what it would demonstrate is that Voltaire had already seen him somewhere, or believed he had, but that he remembered him poorly and so confused him with someone else. That hypothesis regarding Voltaire's intention seems to me most unlikely, however, because it is entirely unnecessary. Voltaire was not confused in the least, and made no mistake in identity at all; he was indeed addressing 'un nommé Rousseau', who was Pierre Rousseau.

The only real mystery in this incident is who told Jean-Jacques about it. Did some troublemaker deliberately give him the impression that Voltaire was angry with him? Did the rumour of the incident spread in such a way that Jean-Jacques's informant was sincere but inaccurate?[13] Or did Jean-Jacques perhaps hear a basically true version, but leap to the conclusion that by 'un nommé Rousseau', Voltaire probably meant him? In view of Jean-Jacques's later tendency to

---

[10] Jean Guéhenno, *Jean-Jacques; en marge des Confessions* (Paris 1948), i.295.
[11] Eugène Ritter, 'Les premières relations entre Voltaire et Rousseau', *Annales Jean-Jacques Rousseau* (1916-1917), xi.60-63: 'A quelle date faut-il placer cette rencontre? Elle est évidemment postérieure à la lettre de Rousseau, que je viens de citer, et qui est du 30 janvier 1750.' Leigh

268, note *a*: 'La lettre de Rousseau à Voltaire du 30 janvier 1750 (no.149) montre que les deux hommes ne s'étaient pas encore rencontrés.'
[12] Collé, *Journal*, i.126.
[13] Desnoiresterres takes Rousseau's sincerity for granted, in *Voltaire*, iii.358.

paranoia, I am inclined to suspect the third case.[14] Whichever it was makes little difference regarding the basic point: the exchange of letters offers no proof that Voltaire did not know Jean-Jacques by sight, only some evidence that Jean-Jacques thought he did not.

It is very true that Rousseau insists in this letter on his hesitation at appearing before Voltaire.[15] Recalling Voltaire's 'bonté et honnêteté' at the time of the *Fêtes de Ramire*, Rousseau observes that 'Un solitaire qui ne sait point parler, un homme timide, découragé, n'osa se présenter à vous. Quel eût été mon titre? Ce ne fut point le Zéle qui me manqua, mais l'orgueil; et n'osant m'offrir à vos yeux, j'attends du tems quelque occasion favorable pour vous témoigner mon respect et ma reconnoissance' (Leigh 149). Later he says, 'Je ne me flatte pas de mériter l'honneur d'être connu de vous . . .' These remarks would appear to rule out any real probability of Voltaire's having seen Rousseau.

Rousseau himself, however, tells us elsewhere that Voltaire had seen him. When Rousseau first came to Paris, in 1742-1743, he was received by several wealthy ladies, among them mme Dupin. Rousseau must have been presented to her in early 1743. By his own account, he fell in love with her on first sight. 'Elle me permit de la venir voir; j'usai, j'abusai de la permission. J'y allois presque tous les jours, j'y dinois deux ou trois fois la semaine' (*Confessions. Œuvres*, i.291). Throughout all this, he was longing to tell the beautiful hostess of his love, but never dared. Several reasons reinforced his natural shyness, including his calculating wish to get ahead, the lady's reserve, and the brilliance of the setting, wherein Jean-Jacques felt he cut a sorry figure.

Sa maison, aussi brillante alors qu'aucune autre dans Paris rassembloit des sociétés auxquelles il ne manquoit que d'être un peu moins nombreuses pour être d'élite dans tous les genres. Elle aimoit à voir tous les gens qui jettoient de l'éclat: les Grands, les gens de lettres, les belles femmes. On ne voyoit chez elle que Ducs, Ambassadeurs, cordons bleus. Mad⁰ la Princesse de Rohan, Mad⁰ la Comtesse de Forcalquier, Mad⁰ de Mirepoix, Mad⁰ de Brignolé, Myladi Hervey pouvoient passer pour ses amies. M. de Fontenelle, l'Abbé de St. Pierre, l'Abbé Sallier, M. de Fourmont, M. de Bernis, M. de Buffon, M. de Voltaire étoient de son cercle et des ses dinés.[16]

[14] I would not agree with Besterman's judgement, however, that Rousseau 'wrote to protest rather peevishly', in *Voltaire*, 3rd ed. (Oxford, Chicago 1976), p.301.

[15] this aspect of the letter led Gaston Maugras to say of it that its 'dignité apparente dissimulait l'excessive humilité', in *Querelles de philosophes: Voltaire et Jean-Jacques Rousseau* (Paris 1886), p.18.

[16] *Confessions, Œuvres*, i.291-2.

In other words, Voltaire and Rousseau must have been together as guests at dinner or at least in the salon of mme Dupin between January and July 1743.[17]

Rousseau, evidently, felt so humbled by this display of talents and titles that he could not believe anyone had noticed him, least of all the great Voltaire. He may of course have been right. Voltaire certainly took no notice of him at the time, and in a sense, that was the only thing that would have counted for Rousseau. He wanted someone who could see the real Rousseau beneath the timid, penurious mask at the far end of the table. In his view, whoever truly saw Rousseau saw a fervent heart, a great destiny, a unique man. What Voltaire saw, and he was skilled at seeing such things, was one more young man from the provinces, wanting to succeed, needing protection and instruction, having talent perhaps. Voltaire usually gave each one some kind of chance, often including financial help, and he expected certain kinds of allegiance and support in return. Anyone with a special interest in Rousseau might have pointed him out to Voltaire – Fontenelle, for example, whom Rousseau had met while presenting his system of music to the Academy, and whom he continued to visit even after he stopped seeing most of his first group of contacts in Paris (*Confessions*, *Œuvres*, i.287). It is even possible that when Voltaire wrote in 1762 that he had once seen Rousseau, it was an artificial memory, produced by some friend who had told him recently that he and his then despised adversary had once dined together.

To sum up, it is certainly not true that Voltaire met Rousseau at mme de Graffigny's salon. Mme de Graffigny did not meet Rousseau herself until until October 1751, by which time Voltaire had left Paris for good. Such slight evidence as there is for the meeting suggests strongly that it had minimal impact on both participants; for neither did it bring about any change in their relationship, which remained at a level of two men of letters who occasionally wrote to each other for a specific purpose. The incident of January 1750, which has been taken as a limit for the earliest possible date of their meeting, does not in reality prove anything. Voltaire made no mistake, but quarrelled with a different Rousseau. Jean-Jacques made the mistake, but gave

---

[17] George R. Havens was kind enough to send me a copy of his article, 'Voltaire's meeting with Rousseau', to appear in *Diderot studies*, in which he reaches the same conclusion as to the time and place of the meeting.

no clue as to the source of his information. He assumed that Voltaire did not know him by sight; but he had in fact been among the guests at mme Dupin's at the same time as Voltaire, in early 1743, and could very well have been seen by Voltaire then. The date Voltaire gave, 1737, is clearly out of the question; 1743 still falls six years shy of the number, but comes closer. Moreover, Voltaire undoubtedly saw mme Dupin frequently in the years before, beginning in the autumn of 1739. There is no reason to suppose that he would recall precisely at what moment Jean-Jacques first appeared, briefly and insignificantly, in a numerous company where Voltaire was a regular star. The meeting between Voltaire and Rousseau was then in all probability not a real introduction, but simply a day when both were in the same room and Voltaire literally 'saw' Rousseau, as he says in his letter, nothing more than that. Rousseau of course recognized the famous Voltaire, and recorded the occasion(s); but he remained convinced that nobody had noticed him, and certainly not the great Voltaire.

IV

Rousseau and mme de Graffigny in 1750-1751

As we have seen, the evidence which was believed to link Rousseau to mme de Graffigny in the first half of 1750 was erroneous. As we will soon see, mme de Graffigny's first meeting with Rousseau took place in October 1751, and her letter on the subject is unequivocal. During the almost two years between the false date and the true one, some significant changes had occurred in the lives of both people. The year 1750 was a pinnacle of success for mme de Graffigny. *Cénie* was in the hands of the Théâtre français and preparations were under way for its première. In the eighteenth century, these preparations entailed frenetic activity on the part of the author, and in the case of a woman author, twice as much effort was required because everything had to be done through agents instead of in person. The actors demanded constant revisions. Frequently they quarrelled over petty matters, and sometimes sulked to force the others to give in. The author would have to resort to the persuasions of friends, or, in cases of irreconcilable disputes, to intervention by the *gentilhomme de la chambre du roi* who was on service at the time. Meanwhile, the author had to organize a favourable claque and take steps to insert good notices into the periodical press. At the same time, rival authors had to be fought off. There was bitter competition for priority in the schedule, and a great deal of concern about good or bad dates for an opening. Mme de Graffigny was convinced that Voltaire was cabaling against her throughout the spring of 1750, and later she claimed that mlle Gaussin had confessed that some stalling had been done at Voltaire's behest. In any case, *Cénie* had to open in June, not generally regarded as the best time; it was outside the main season, which ran from the *rentrée* in November until about Easter, the weather was hot, and the theatre frequently uncomfortable. It was the time of the year for new actors to try out, and for unknown playwrights. As it happened, *Cénie* triumphed over all these handicaps, and drew large enough crowds to warrant a continuation into the regular season in the late autumn.

Rousseau during this period was still a completely unknown figure. In July, just after the opening of *Cénie*, he learned that he had won first prize at Dijon, and his friend the abbé Raynal solicited something from him for the *Mercure* and received *L'Allée de Silvie*, which came out in September. During those same months, the pages of the *Mercure* were filled with verse compliments to the author of *Cénie* from writers like Nivelle de La Chaussée and mme Du Boccage, and letters on *Cénie* from M. Olivier, and La Font de Saint-Yenne. Rousseau no doubt went to see *Cénie* and must have been aware of the clamour surrounding it; but mme de Graffigny understandably did not notice these first signs of Rousseau's success.

The revival of *Cénie* did not provoke as much drama in mme de Graffigny's life as had the first presentation. Nevertheless its continued popularity led to a flurry of invitations, many of them from the great noble families. Moreover, the printed text came off Duchesne's presses during the winter, and mme de Graffigny sent off dozens of gift copies to friends and protectors. Even the staging finally produced some excitement; the run ended because one of the actors, Roselli, was killed in a duel by another actor. By that time, the success was well enough established so that mme de Graffigny was not personally disappointed but it did upset her routine for a time.

This was, of course, the moment when Rousseau's first *Discours* appeared in print, and overnight he became famous. Diderot's exuberant letter to Rousseau, who was ill in bed at the time, wherein he claimed that 'il n'y a pas d'exemple d'un succés pareil' (*Confessions*, *Œuvres*, i.363), is not echoed in mme de Graffigny's reports to Devaux on the literary scene in Paris. She was still too much preoccupied with her own affairs. The publication of the *Discours* does, however, mark the first mention of Rousseau in her letters. The letter is dated 31 January 1751, and is a response to Devaux's commentary on Rousseau; he had read the excerpts in the January *Mercure*, and wrote to mme de Graffigny as follows:

Je viens d'achever le Mercure,[1] chere amie, et je veux, moi, vous parler de deux ou trois morceaux dont l'un m'a enchanté, en me faisant jetter a la lettre des cris de fureur, et d'indignation. Ne vous avisés pas d'en penser autrement que moy, car je serois capable d'en etre furieux meme contre vous. Entendés-vous que je veux parler de ce discours qui a remporté le prix a l'academie de Dijon? Je ne puis pardonner a ce Mr Rousseau de

[1] the excerpts had been published in the *Mercure* (janvier 1751), pp.98-116.

defendre avec tant d'esprit et d'eloquence une chose qui me revolte. Je ne suis pas cruel, mais je voudrois le tenir lié et garotté et avoir le plaisir de le fustiger jusqu'a ce qu'il se dedise. Alors je le baiserois, je le caresserois, je l'adorerois. Connoissés-vous dans ce genre quelque chose d'aussi beau, d'aussi eloquent, que cet indigne discours? N'y a-t-il pas de quoy en mourir de depit? Ma colere est egale a mon admiration. Si j'ay jamais eu envie d'ecrire, c'est dans ce moment-cy, mais si j'ay jamais eté decouragé c'est aussi dans ce moment. Comment laissés triompher ce maudit Suisse, mais comment oser luy disputer la victoire? Je me tairai, c'est plus tost fait, mais en verité j'enrage. Vous riés sans doute de mon fanatisme et moy je suis revolté de votre froideur si vous ne le partagés pas.[2]

Mme de Graffigny replied:

Par la raison que je suis moins fan[atique] que toi je ne veux ny etrangler ny foetter Mr Rousseau, mais a quelques degré pres je pense comme toi. J'aime assés ce que lui a dit Thieri. C'est mon medecin lorrain. Rousseau est son ami. Il lui a donné son œuvre. Thieri lui a dit, 'Mon ami, je vais metre ton discour au fond d'un coffre d'ou je ne le tirerai de 20 ans. Je veux encore aimer les arts pendant ce tems la.'[3]

Thieri was François Thierry, a fairly well known doctor, who is mentioned several times in the *Confessions*. Despite his being from Lorraine, mme de Graffigny had just met him a few weeks earlier. Rousseau says of him in book viii: 'Le seul de mes amis à qui j'eus intérest de m'ouvrir fut le medecin Thyerri, qui soigna ma pauvre tante dans une de ses couches où elle se trouva fort mal' (*Œuvres* i.358), and 'Je vis successivement Morand, Daran, Helvetius, Malouin, Thyerri, qui tous très savans, tous mes amis, me traitèrent chacun à sa mode, ne me soulagérent point, et m'affoiblirent considérablement' (i.365). If Thierry told any other stories about Rousseau, mme de Graffigny did not pass them on to Devaux. It should be noted in passing that from the very beginning, mme de Graffigny disagreed with Rousseau; despite the similarities we can see between her works and his, similarities observed by Iselin in 1752, as I mentioned earlier, she felt herself a part of the world of Voltaire, not in revolt against it. Indeed, she seems to have shared the

[2] 28 January 1751 (GP, liii.97-8). The Graffigny papers include Devaux's letters to mme de Graffigny up to July 1751, but not thereafter.

[3] 31 January 1751 (GP, l.51). The paper is torn as shown.

common reaction – evident also in Devaux's remarks and Thierry's *boutade* – that Rousseau was not really sincere. This initial spark of interest might have led mme de Graffigny to seek out Rousseau, and evidently she did not lack for intermediaries who could have carried an invitation. Despite the closing of *Cénie*, however, mme de Graffigny remained extremely occupied with her own affairs. Her enhanced reputation led Duchesne to ask for some additional letters for a new edition of *Les Lettres d'une Péruvienne*, a task she worked on in the early months of 1751. Meanwhile, she was beset with suitors, some of them no doubt spurred on by her glory: her lodger, a lawyer named Valleré; another lawyer, an elderly long-time acquaintance named Blaru; the young writer Bret; the abbé Turgot, seeking comfort after the death of his father. The guests at her salon were more numerous than ever. In July, she moved from her old house on the rue Saint Hyacinthe to a new one in the rue d'Enfer, with many complications; the search was long and slow, the negotiations on the lease complicated, and the repairs extensive and often delayed. The main event of the year, however, was the marriage of her ward, Minette de Ligniville, to Helvétius, celebrated on 17 August after some five years of negotiations and delays, which reached a peak of intensity in early 1751.[4] By the autumn, however, calm had returned at last, and mme de Graffigny could begin to enjoy the benefits of her fame.

Rousseau in the meanwhile had become an authentic celebrity. If Devaux characteristically never summoned up the energy to refute Rousseau's *Discours*, a great many less indolent readers wrote and published a series of refutations and responses. In September 1751 the *Mercure* printed an anonymous refutation whose author was none other than Stanislas, king of Poland and ruler of Lorraine, and whose identity did not long remain secret. The following month the *Mercure* printed Rousseau's reply, and yet another refutation by yet another Lorrainer, the abbé Gautier, for whom mme de Graffigny had recently tried and failed to get a permission to print a work defending Christi-

---

[4] mme Helvétius became a well known salon hostess, and many accounts of her life are available. Peter Allan has prepared an edition of her letters, including those in the Graffigny papers; presumably they will be published as part of the *Correspondance complète* of Helvétius, which has been prepared under the direction of David W. Smith of the University of Toronto. This edition will include excerpts from mme de Graffigny's letters, and will certainly be the authoritative work on Helvétius and his wife.

anity against an anonymous critic; everyone agreed that the abbé Gautier had the last word but not the best of the argument. For these reasons, mme de Graffigny's curiosity about Rousseau was perhaps even greater than most. Nonetheless, in writing to Devaux she claimed to have invited him at the request of a friend, whom she calls 'ma Comtesse'; this was the countess of Sandwich, an elderly English lady who had been living in Paris for many years. The meeting took place on Thursday, 28 October 1751, and was related in a letter written the following day:

Je fis hier connoissance avec ce Rousseau qui devient si celebre par son paradoxe et par sa reponce a votre roi.[5] Ma Comtesse[6] vouloit le voir. Je le menai diner chez elle.[7] C'est un drole de philosophe, il est habillé presque de bure, coeffé comme Harmand,[8] point d'epée quoi qu'en habit de couleur, enfin le plus ridiculement qu'il peut. Mais ses discours ne sont guere analogue a son vetement. C'est une legereté, une facilité, une gentillesse a comparer presque a celle de Voltaire. Il vous jette mille petites louanges dans son espece de volubilité que vous ramassez si vous voulez mais que vous pouvez laisser tomber sans embaras. Il a un son de voix et un[e] facilité de parler qui jette beaucoup d'agrement sur ses discours. Tout ce qu'il dit est bien ecrit. Sa figure est chetive, mais il a une phisionomie comme celle de ces enfants que l'on apelle eveillés, les yeux noir rond mais vif comme les escarboucle. Tout cela n'est pas joli mais cela plait. Il eut bien de l'esprit, et la Comtesse aussi. Mais il est si fanatique de son sisteme et il met si fort l'evangile au dessus de tous les autres livres que l'on n'ose contredire l'un de peur de l'offencer et l'autre de peur de s'offencer soi-meme.[9]

On the whole, mme de Graffigny's account confirms what Rousseau said of himself in the *Confessions*. This was the time when Rousseau's notoriety made him a prize for the hostesses of Paris (*Œuvres*, i.367). The countess of Sandwich's aristocratic curiosity illustrates that lionzation as well as it could be done. Rousseau spoke of his dress in these terms: 'Je commençai ma réforme par ma parure; je quittai la dorure et les bas blancs, je pris une perruque ronde, je posai l'épée,

---

[5] *Discours sur les sciences et les arts* (*Œuvres*, iii.1-30) and *Observations de Jean-Jacques Rousseau, de Genève, sur la réponse qui à été faite à son discours* (*Œuvres*, iii.35-7).
[6] the countess of Sandwich; see G. E. Cokayne, *The Complete peerage* (London 1949), xi.434.
[7] she lived on the rue Vaugirard, in the

former house of mme de Lafayette, according to mme de Graffigny; it would be number 50 today.
[8] Armand-François Haquet, called Armand (1699-1765), comic actor at the Théâtre français.
[9] to Devaux, 29 October 1751 (GP, lvi.135).

je vendis ma montre, en me disant avec une joye incroyable: Grace au Ciel, je n'aurai plus besoin de savoir l'heure qu'il est' (*Confessions*, *Œuvres*, i.363). Mme de Graffigny plainly was not impressed by the reform; the 'Harmand' to whom she compares Rousseau was an actor at the Théâtre français who specialized in comic figures.

Rousseau himself admitted the haphazard and incongruous nature of this reform, when he wrote, 'Quelque austére que fut ma reforme somptuaire, je ne l'étendis pas d'abord jusqu'à mon linge, qui étoit beau et en quantité, reste de mon équipage de Venise, et pour lequel j'avois un attachement particulier' (*Œuvres*, i.364). When this linen was finally stolen, in December 1751, the police made a list of the missing items, and most were shirts. If Rousseau was wearing one at the time of their meeting, mme de Graffigny apparently did not notice it; she was struck more by the rough quality of the outer garments and the grotesque mixtures of styles and social codes. Perhaps one of those fancy shirts contributed subliminally to mme de Graffigny's overall impression. As far as his appearance and conduct were concerned, Rousseau was projecting the image of an eccentric, not of a systematic reformer or thinker.

If Rousseau has glossed over the degree to which he must have seemed merely mad to his contemporaries in those respects, he has exaggerated in the other direction with regard to his speech. In the *Confessions* he dwells at length on his bearish behaviour in polite society:

Jetté malgré moi dans le monde sans en avoir le ton, sans être en état de le prendre et de m'y pouvoir assujettir, je m'avisai d'en prendre un à moi qui m'en dispensât. Ma sote et maussade timidité que je ne pouvois vaincre ayant pour principe la crainte de manquer aux bienséances, je pris pour m'enhardir le parti de les fouler aux pieds. Je me fis cynique et caustique par honte; j'affectai de mépriser la politesse que je ne savois pas pratiquer.[10]

The psychological mechanism here described has been verified by modern social scientists a hundred times over. Furthermore, Rousseau certainly did commit some boorish acts and speak some loutish words; but the evidence would suggest that he began to do so with frequency and with forethought somewhat later than the autumn of 1751 where the *Confessions* appear to place that change. And he was by no means

[10] *Confessions*, *Œuvres*, i.368.

as incapable of doing otherwise as he liked to remember. Even within the *Confessions* there is much to hint that Rousseau spoke with great charm, especially about himself; from mme de Warens to mme Dupin, he won the sympathy of almost every lady he met by telling the story of his life. True, that is not exactly the same thing as the usual social banter, and would not be appropriate in all situations. It is certainly not what mme de Graffigny was describing; but mme d'Epinay offers a similar portrait of Rousseau in the *Histoire de mme de Montbrillant*: 'Il est complimenteur sans être poli, ou du moins sans en avoir l'air. Il est sans les usages du monde; mais il est aisé de voir qu'il a infiniment d'esprit.'[11] Madame d'Epinay put more emphasis on the lack of usual manners than did mme de Graffigny, but at bottom their impression was the same: Rousseau had both wit and seductive charm for the perceptive listener, especially female; but his manner was unconventional.

The irony is that Rousseau's eccentricities, although they arose from a sincere rejection of society, seemed to the members of society just another gambit. Even rudeness could be an asset; Versac had laid out for Meilcour a whole plan of social conquest based on that principle. Versac, however, broke rules he had mastered to perfection; and he understood in minute detail what effect he was creating and what response he was getting. Rousseau, on the other hand, frequently miscalculated, and his successes could be as disconcerting as his failures. At the very moment when he was labouring to free himself from social evils, long coveted in vain but now renounced, society suddenly lionized him. Mme de Graffigny's evaluation of Rousseau, even though it runs contrary to the view most people hold today, probably represents a typical contemporary impression in 1751. Comparing him to Voltaire, she thinks of him as a rival, not as a being from a different world, which was Rousseau's view of himself. In the months that followed this first meeting, Rousseau sustained his role and in the end alienated mme de Graffigny; she felt, evidently, that having accepted his gambit, she was entitled to accede to a higher level of communication with him. Their masks ought to have been lowered, and they should have laughed at the public, comic Rousseau.

[11] mme d'Epinay, *Histoire de mme de Montbrillant*, ed. Georges Roth (Paris 1951), i.520.

The only comment on Rousseau's ideas appears in the final sentence. It will surprise no one that Rousseau was an ardent defender of his own system, nor that the inspiration of the first *Discours* had taken on enough extension and consistency to be called a system. He was in the heat of the polemical battles, which everyone recognizes provided the impetus, if any was needed, for Rousseau to pursue his thought to its ultimate limits. It would be dangerous to put too much faith in mme de Graffigny's judgement on this point anyway; she was responsive to fashions but not a rigorous thinker herself.

Rousseau's enthusiasm for the Gospel, on the other hand, touches a vexed question. Although he tries to minimize his irresponsibility, in the *Confessions* Rousseau makes clear that his religious convictions depended largely on convenience from the time he fled Geneva. Scholars, in verifying the outlines of the story, have uncovered evidence that Rousseau cast off his Calvinism with less reluctance than he said, and there is very little to suggest any profound religious concern, much less faith, between the abjuration in April 1728 and the moment of which we are speaking. By contrast, it is obvious that in the late 1750s Rousseau took upon himself, with complete sincerity, the function of religious apologist among his atheistic former friends like Diderot and d'Holbach. The debate, then, focuses on the date of the awakening, or reawakening, of his religious sensibility.

An incident which would seem to mark a turning point is his reintegration into the church of Geneva, in August 1754. Without attempting to decide the subtle question of whether a 'conversion' occurred then, or not until the end of his four-month stay in Geneva, or perhaps not until 1762 as the Pléiade editors suggest (*Œuvres*, i.1456), we can say at least that by this time the process of conversion was under way. For many, this process seems to have begun only a short time before, at least in any explicit and overt fashion. Obviously, the religious conversion can always be taken as an eventual implication of the reform that certainly started with the illumination of Vincennes. The question is not, however, the subconscious evolution of his faith, nor even the possible conscious but private thoughts he might have had on the subject; rather, the question is when the religious theme emerged as a significant element in his system.

Because the religious quarrel became a central issue in the break between Rousseau and the encyclopedists, it has been assumed plausibly enough that the emergence of the religious element and the collapse of the old friendships would run in parallel. Moreover, those allies-turned-enemies have provided an account of their first awareness of Rousseau's feelings. In mme d'Epinay's novel *Histoire de mme de Montbrillant*, Rousseau is depicted at a dinner at mlle Quinault's salon, in the company of Saint-Lambert and Duclos, among others.[12] A discussion of religion arises, in which most of the company openly scoff at the notion of God, until Rousseau bursts out in an impassioned declaration of his faith. It has long been realized that mme d'Epinay's work is fiction, despite a certain number of authentic letters. It belongs to the genre of autobiographical fiction, though, and the first editors made bold to assume that it was a *roman à clef*, true in all details except for the pseudonyms. Therefore they inserted the real names and published the work as the *Mémoires de mme d'Epinay*.[13] The scene at mlle Quinault's, or more accurately, mme Médéric's as she is named in the novel, seems to have been a late addition, attributable mostly to Diderot; for when Rousseau returned to Paris from his exile, Diderot, Grimm, and mme d'Epinay feared the effects of his *Confessions*, and they rewrote mme d'Epinay's manuscript to counter-attack. Needless to say, the character of Rousseau, or rather René, is portrayed as a villain. Much of the novel is easily identifiable as fiction, some of it invented for purely polemical reasons. In fairness to the authors of this hoax, they did not in fact bring it before the public at all, once it became clear that Rousseau would not be allowed to publish his *Confessions*. It is the nineteenth-century editor who must bear the blame for the mischief; not only did he bring it to light, but also he eliminated as much as possible of whatever would have identified it as a novel.

In spite of so much to undermine its authority, it has been supposed that the dinner at mme Médéric's must have some basis in reality, that Diderot reconstituted more or less accurately an incident that had happened. Rousseau says in the *Confessions* that he was introduced to mlle Quinault's by Duclos, and his entry can be dated between 15 April 1754, and June of the same year (*Œuvres*, i.387, 1450-51). Thus it would appear that Rousseau's friends first learned of his

---

[12] *ibid.*, ii.400-415.
[13] see the introduction by Georges Roth, i.i-xlii.

newfound faith in God shortly before his trip to Geneva. It must be pointed out, however, that even in the *Histoire de mme de Montbrillant* that chronology cannot work; the other dates would seem to call for Rousseau's profession of faith to take place in September 1751 – a date remarkably close to the time when mme de Graffigny remarked on his enthusiasm for the Gospel.

The dinner at mme Médéric's ought to be appreciated for what it is – one of Diderot's philosophical dialogues – but distrusted as biographical information on Rousseau. Like many another fictional incident, the scene is composed of real details. One might hazard the guess that the vehement praise of the Gospel that struck mme de Graffigny had also stayed in Diderot's mind, so that the ideas and even the tone attributed to René-Rousseau are, in that sense, real. Rousseau's presence at mlle Quinault's is equally real, attested to by Rousseau himself; but it comes from a different moment in his life. Rousseau's sudden outburst in the midst of a convivial dinner could well be the transposition of yet another scene, related both by Grimm and d'Holbach, where Rousseau denounced his friends' mystification of a curate named Petit (*Œuvres*, i.1450). That scene took place at about the right time – 3 February 1754 – but of course lacks the philosophical relevance and furthermore casts Rousseau's friends in a somewhat unsavoury role.

Since the dinner at mme Médéric's constitutes the only important evidence for a late, and suspect, conversion on Rousseau's part, the case for a strong surge of religious feeling in late 1751 becomes very coherent. The first *Discours* had been predominantly, indeed almost exclusively, based on examples from Greek and Roman antiquity. The first bit that came to Rousseau on the road to Vincennes was the 'prosopopée de Fabricius', and the natural sources for his vision of an uncorrupted society are Sparta and the Roman republic. Not long after, Rousseau wrote an essay on the virtues of heroes, following the classical tradition and citing mainly ancient Greeks and Romans.[14] At about the same time, he composed a *Parallèle entre Socrate et Caton*, only recently rediscovered and published; the two classical heroes of the title seem to exemplify the two possible types of heroic virtue.[15]

---

[14] *Discours sur la vertu du héros*, in *Œuvres*, iii.1262-74.

[15] Claude Pichois and René Pintard, *Jean-Jacques entre Socrate et Caton* (Paris 1972).

There is but one reference to the Gospel in the first *Discours*, and a reckless one it is. In a footnote near the end, Rousseau discusses the destruction of the library in Alexandria by the caliph Omar, to support his attack on printing. Concluding the note, he writes: 'Cependant, supposez Grégoire le Grand à la place d'Omar et l'Evangile à la place de l'Alcoran, la Bibliothèque auroit encore été brulée, et ce seroit peut-être le plus beau trait de la vie de cet Illustre Pontife' (*Œuvres*, iii.28). In the right context, Voltaire or Diderot might have penned the sentence as a proof of the fanaticism of all religions. In this context, however, one must read the final clause without irony. Rousseau, aware of a tension within Christianity between a worldly and accommodating church and a fundamentalist and obscurantist tradition, chose the latter.

One sentence in a footnote would not suffice to make that case persuasively. It was in fact in refuting king Stanislas, in September 1751, that Rousseau openly and explicitly declared his stand on the matter. The passage on Christianity is several pages long. Rousseau defends himself against the charge of wanting to suppress the study of religion, but goes on to argue that science and learning have corrupted the pure and simple faith of the first Christians. Heresies, schisms, intolerance, and persecution are all, according to Rousseau, the results of having introduced the arts and sciences into the realm of faith. Near the end of this section of his response, he writes: 'Les Sciences sont florissantes aujourd'hui, la Littérature et les Arts brillent parmi nous; quel profit en a tiré la Religion? Demandons-le à cette multitude de Philosophes qui se piquent de n'en point avoir' (*Œuvres*, iii.48), or again, 'Ce divin Livre [l'Evangile], le seul nécessaire à un Chrétien, et le plus utile de tous à quiconque même ne le seroit pas, n'a besoin que d'être médité pour porter dans l'ame l'amour de son Auteur, et la volonté d'accomplir ses préceptes' (*Œuvres*, iii.48-9). Both the tone and the import of these remarks are unmistakable.

Rousseau's enthusiasms had the intermittent qualities of most strong feelings. Utterly sincere and never entirely absent, they nonetheless cannot remain for long at their peaks of intensity. By December, when Rousseau began meditating his reply to Borde, the religious theme seems to have been subordinated again to the discussion of classical antiquity. Cato emerges there as a key figure, and as we shall see, that obsession links Rousseau to mme de Graffigny. It seems probable that even Rousseau's intimate friends, like Diderot, mistook this outburst of Christian fervour for a temporary manic aberration. As a polemical device, the recourse to the Gospel was brilliant; devout adversaries, of whom king Stanislas was one, were trapped in the dilemma, and had no effective answer to Omar's logic. He conceded himself beaten in the debate, but went ahead with his patronage of the arts and sciences which made Nancy one of the glories of Enlightenment culture. Rousseau, on the other hand, felt himself committed to his ideas as no one else did; and in the long run he had to pay the price for it.

It is not possible to say with certainty when mme de Graffigny saw Rousseau for the second time. In November, she sent Devaux a copy of Rousseau's reply to the abbé Gautier, and later mocked Gautier's desire to publish a rejoinder.[16] She reacted much more positively to Borde's discourse, which was published in the *Mercure* in December.[17] None of these allusions leads to any mention of Rousseau himself, however, and their next certain meeting is described in a letter dated 30 December 1751:

A propos j'eus hier matin la visite de Jean Jaques Rousseau (comme il dit). Il me mit tout a fait au fait de l'auteur du discour de Lion.[18] Il s'apelle Mr de Borde,[19] il est fort de la connoissance de Jean Jaques, de celle de Duclos, de Mr de Fontenelle, ami intime de l'abbé de Mabli.[20] En un mot ce n'est ny un fantome ny un homme a etre prete-nom. Ainci tu peux effacer lui de ton catalogue au moins pour cet article.[21]

The first sentence sounds as though this was his first visit since their meeting in October. The passage is otherwise very uninformative, but revealing for that very reason. It is clear that for mme de Graffigny, Rousseau meant no more – indeed, almost certainly less – than her

---

[16] 21 November 1751 (GP, lvi.70); 3 December 1751 (GP, lvi.185); 13 December 1751 (GP, lvi.200).

[17] 17 December 1751 (GP, lvi.203).

[18] *Discours sur les avantages des sciences et des arts, prononcé dans l'assemblée publique de l'Académie des sciences et belles-lettres de Lyon, le 22 Juin 1751*, published anonymously in the *Mercure* (décembre 1751), i.25-64.

[19] Charles Borde (1711-1781); on his relations with Rousseau see the *Confessions* (*Œuvres*, i.280 and n6; i.366 and n2).

[20] Charles Pinot Duclos (1704-1772), Bernard Le Bovier de Fontenelle (1657-1757) and the abbé Gabriel Bonnot de Mably (1709-1785) were all well known and so served to identify Borde. Mably was from Lyons like Borde; it was he who gave Rousseau a letter for Fontenelle around 1742. On their relations with Rousseau, see the *Confessions* (*Œuvres*, i.280 and n2, n4; i.371 and n1).

[21] mme de Graffigny to Devaux (GP, lvi.224).

other guests, like Duclos, who was a regular member of her group, besides being an established author and academician. Mme de Graffigny was not close to Fontenelle, but knew him. Compared to them, and even to herself, Rousseau was a minor celebrity in 1751. She therefore exploited him primarily for literary gossip to send on to Devaux in Lunéville; in this case, Borde's reply to Rousseau's *Discours* was a timely topic, and Rousseau's identification of its author was apparently the only thing that she retained of his visit.

Not long afterwards, on 9 January 1752, mme de Graffigny wrote to Devaux that Rousseau wanted to reply to Borde, and that she had advised him, through the intermediary of Duclos, not to:

Je vais achever de repondre a ta letre avant que l'autre n'arrive. Jean Jaques Rousseau grate son oreille quand on lui parle du discours de Mr de Borde et non pas La Borde. Il vouloit cependant y faire une espece de reponce indirecte comme il l'ataque indirectement, mais je lui ai fait dire de la part de Gormas[22] que s'il ecrivoit encore sur cette matiere il perdoit toute sa gloire et qu'il retomboit dans la classe des petits grimaults qui ne veulent jamais laisser le dernier [mot][23] aux autres. Je ne sais s'il se taira. Non, le discours du Mercure n'est point trop fêté. Je n'en ai rien entendu dire qu'a nos amis letrés. Encore la plus part ne l'ont pas lus.[24]

Mme de Graffigny's advice was partly motivated by the fact that she agreed with Borde far more than with Rousseau. In fact, she entered the Académie française prize competition of 1752, with a discourse which was apparently an indirect attack on Rousseau's first *Discours*. She moaned to Devaux, 'Mr de Borde m'a bien volé mais qu'importe, je ne me decourage pas. Je prendrai un autre tour pour dire peutetre les memes choses et cela sufira'.[25]

Needless to say, Rousseau had no reason to take mme de Graffigny's advice, and did not; his reply to Borde appeared in April 1752 (*Œuvres*, iii.71-96). Mme de Graffigny read it soon after it appeared, and wrote to Devaux:

Je lus hier soir la reponce de Jean Jaques Rousseau a Mr de Borde. Il m'a annimé a dire le contraire.[26] Peu s'en faut que je ne sois aussi en colere contre lui que toi. Cette derniere reponce ne montre que le fanatisme le plus outré. J'ai besoin de me rapeler mes motifs de compation pour lui pour

---

[22] pseudonym of Duclos.
[23] omitted by mistake.
[24] GP, lviii.17.

[25] 14 January 1752 (GP, lviii.24).
[26] that is, in her own discourse.

retenir mon indignation. Mais il est si malheureux que je lui passe tout. Primo il a une cause de mort en lui qui outre des douleurs presque continuelles lui donne la certitude de ne point guerir et de ne pas vivre six ans. Ce sont des champignons dans la vessie. En second lieu il a perdu son bien par l'injustice des homme et il a essuié des perfidies singulieres. Il etoit chez mr Du Pin non pas demeurant mais entretenus.[27] Apparement qu'il y a essuié des desagremens. Il est a present dans un gregnier ou il est copiste pour vivre. Pense donc au peu de profit et au degout insuportables que doit avoir un homme comme lui de copier tant de miserables productions des premiers sots qui voudroient l'employer. Pour moi je ne sais rien de si malheureux que lui dans l'univer. Et rien qui le merite moins. C'est la probité la plus rigide, les vertus les plus mâles et l'esprit le plus universel. On repete a present un balet dont il a fait la musique et les paroles.[28] Ses amis l'ont forcé de le faire jouer. Au moins cela lui donnera de quoi mourir. Hais-le apres cela si tu l'ose. Hais-le pour le seul defaut que tu posede au supreme degré – le fanatisme. Oh je te haïrois bien toi si tu ne pensois pas sagement a son egard.[29]

It is clear from this letter that mme de Graffigny had come to know much more about Rousseau than before, but it is impossible to say with certainty whether she had heard it from him personally or from his friends. She had seen Duclos at least six different times since the first of the year, and he was very close to Rousseau at this time. According to the *Confessions*, it was Duclos who arranged for a special anonymous rehearsal of *Le Devin du village* shortly after it was completed. Mme de Graffigny's allusion to *Le Devin* is the earliest known, and requires its conception and composition to be dated somewhat sooner than has usually been supposed. The inspiration for it came during a visit of eight or ten days at Passy, and the whole work was finished within three weeks, by Rousseau's account. Assuming that Duclos began arranging for the rehearsal immediately, and told mme de Graffigny at the same time, the stay with Mussard in Passy can have been no later than mid-March; and an earlier date is obviously plausible, for Rousseau's activities during this period are otherwise unknown. The other facts cited by mme de Graffigny confirm what is already

---

[27]Rousseau relates his connections with the Dupin family in books vii and viii of the *Confessions*; regarding the date of his departure from their employ, see the notes to Leigh 157, 160, 177 and 180.

[28] *Le Devin du village* (*Œuvres*, ii.1093-1114); Rousseau tells the story of its composition and performance in the *Confessions* (*Œuvres*, i.374-83). See also Leigh 173.

[29] 12 April 1752 (GP, lviii.158).

well known about Rousseau's health, poverty, and character; and it is clear that his reputation, or myth, was becoming widely known.

Mme de Graffigny sent copies of the reply to Borde to Devaux,[30] and then Rousseau's name disappeared from her letters again until the summer. That does not mean that he never came to her house; rather, he had been assimilated into that large band of young writers like Bret who made up the regular circle of guests. Bret, in fact, has left an account of Rousseau's appearance in mme de Graffigny's circle; it was first published in 1952 by A. C. Keys, and more recently in the *Correspondance* of Rousseau (Leigh, ii.310-13: appendice A81):

J'étois très lié vers 1750 avec la célèbre Mad^e de Graffigny qui m'avoit honoré de son amitié et chez laquelle je passois alors une partie de ma Vie dans un cercle distingué d'hommes de lettres Et de Grands. Mr Rousseau y fut présenté par son ami Mr Duclos. Quoique toujours modeste, toujours intérieur Et ne se livrant à la conversation Et aux divers amusemens de la société qu'avec une réserve infinie, je l'y ai quelquefois vu trés aimable Et même une fois de la plus ingénieuse coquetterie. En tout il n'Etoit question que de l'interresser un peu: une demoiselle Etrangere, fille de beaucoup d'Esprit, marchant déja vers son Eté mais d'une physionomie ouverte Et riante et dont la conversation animée sembloit encore plus piquante par un joli accent italien, attaqua un jour particulièrement notre philosophe dont elle Entrevoyait sans doute la secrete sensibilité au fond de cet œil d'aigle qu'il portoit souvent sur Elle, Et dont le feu devenoit toujours plus brulant lorsqu'il s'abandonnoit à la nature et à ses sens.

Mlle Bagarotti ne s'etoit point trompée. Mr Rousseau sortit pour ainsi dire de lui même, se developpa Et s'embellit à nos yeux, mille traits agréables lui Echapèrent, il fut bien secondé, et je me rappelle Encore avec Etonnement tout le changement que fit en lui ce désir momentané de plaire car cet incident n'eut point de suite, mais Pendant 2 ou 3 heures il nous offrit notre philosophe avec un déployement de Grâces qu'on ne lui soupçonnoit pas Et que lui auroit envié le courtisan le plus avantageux et le plus accoutumé à triompher dans ces Especes de joutes Galantes. C'est dans cette disposition d'esprit qu'il a probablement tracé ces pages brulantes où son ame s'est Répandue avec toute la sensibilité dont elle Etoit remplie.

Bret did not record these impressions until 1785, more than thirty years after they occurred; some errors of detail do not, I think, give cause to doubt the basic accuracy of what he says. Bret himself became

---

[30] 12 April 1752 (GP, lviii.160); 14 April 1752 (GP, lviii.162).

mme de Graffigny's friend and suitor, although by her account never her lover, immediately following the success of *Cénie* in the summer of 1750; in 1751 and 1752 they were still very close, and their liaison had suffered no interruption. The date 'vers 1750' is therefore accurate in Bret's terms. Duclos is not mentioned by mme de Graffigny as having brought Rousseau to her, but he had been one of her most assiduous visitors and most trusted advisors for almost ten years. They met through mlle Quinault, and Duclos had helped pilot *Cénie* through the whole difficult process from conception to staging. It is thus quite possible that when mme de Graffigny wanted to invite Rousseau, at the request of the countess of Sandwich, Duclos conveyed the invitation. Mlle Bagarotti seems not to be mentioned in mme de Graffigny's letters until the summer of 1754, when she appears first as 'mon Italienne'. That epithet would indicate that mme de Graffigny expected Devaux to know her, but apparently he did not, because on 11 July 1754, mme de Graffigny wrote to explain who she was: daughter of a general, about forty years old, under the care of the empress since her father's death, living on a pension in Paris because the empress wanted to prevent her from marrying count Kinski.[31] According to mme de Graffigny, she had been in Paris for two years, and so her presence at mme de Graffigny's salon in 1752 is quite plausible.

It was in June 1752 that Isaak Iselin noted links between Rousseau and mme de Graffigny in his diary. Her first mention of him was in a letter of 13 June 1752:

J'ai passé la plus grande partie de mon apres diner avec un Suisse de 25 ans qui en sait plus qu'un accademicien françois. Ah, mon Dieu, ou le gout se va-t-il loger! Il a pris une fausse enseigne pour voir la mere de Cenie et de Zilia[32] en me disant qu'il venoit me faire des complimens de Mr Hubert[33] et puis il m'a avoué que ce n'etoit pas vray, que Hubert n'avoit pas l'esprit de penser que l'on eut envie de me voir.[34]

---

[31] 11 July 1754 (GP, lxi.221).
[32] heroines of mme de Graffigny's works.
[33] the editor of Iselin's diary says this was Wernhard Huber (1700-1755), a scholar from Basel; but someone in the family of Martin Huber (1682-1732), an agent of the duke of Lorraine, seems a more likely candidate. See the *Dictionnaire historique et biographique de la Suisse*, iv. 172.
[34] to Devaux (GP, lviii.265).

V

Les Saturnales: history

In the same letter where mme de Graffigny first tells of Iselin's visits, she also mentions the need to write a new playlet to send to Vienna:

Je ne saurois travailler, mon ami, causons. C'est a ma petite piece pour Viene qui j'ai comencée mais qui n'est pas encore en train. Il faut pourtant qu'elle soit partie au mois de septembre et je n'ai pas beaucoup de matinée a donner au travail pendant l'eté. Nous verons. Si elle n'est pas faite on ne me fera pas pendre.[1]

Since the late 1740s writing playlets for the emperor had been one of mme de Graffigny's major sources of income. After the success of *Les Lettres d'une Péruvienne* had made her a fashionable author, the emperor, the former duke of Lorraine, paid her a pension in return for a regular supply of edifying dramatic works to be performed by the imperial children. Two of these plays, *Ziman et Zenise* and *Azor* were published posthumously and are thus available in mme de Graffigny's *Œuvres complètes*, of which there were several editions in the late eighteenth and early nineteenth centuries. The titles of several others are known, because of their presence in prince Khevenhüller-Metsch's diaries, for example, or allusions in various letters in the Noël family papers or elsewhere.[2] Such was, for example, *Le Temple de la vertu*, which Iselin heard read,[3] and which Prévost alluded to in dedicating his translation of *Clarissa* to Mme de Graffigny.[4] As this letter suggests, mme de Graffigny did not take this chore very seriously, and frequently besought her literary acquaintances for help in finding a subject or in writing the dialogue or in copying or punctuating.

---

[1] to Devaux, 12 June 1752 (GP, lviii. 259).

[2] Fürsten Johann Josef Khevenhüller-Metsch, *Aus der Zeit Maria Theresias: Tagebuch 1742-1767* (Wien 1907-1917).

[3] Iselin, pp.147, 148.

[4] abbé Antoine François Prévost, tr., Samuel Richardson, *Lettres angloises, ou histoire de miss Clarisse Harlowe* (Londres 1751): 'Si j'étois dans l'usage de mettre un nom célèbre à la tête de mes livres, mon choix ne seroit pas incertain. Grandeurs, richesses, vous n'obtiendriez pas mon hommage. Je supplierois l'illustre auteur de *Cénie* et des *Lettres Péruviennes* d'adopter *Clarisse Harlove*. L'aimable famille; Un lieu chéri du ciel, qui rassembleroit *Zilia*, *Cénie*, et *Clarisse*, sous les ailes de cette excellente mère, seroit le temple de la *Vertu* et du *Sentiment*'.

Many, like *Ziman* and *Azor*, are fairy tales; others dramatize incidents from the life of the emperor; all have a strong moral tone in the sentimental mode designed to inculcate virtue and kindness into the young Marie-Antoinette and her siblings.

On 18 June mme de Graffigny wrote to Devaux that she had completed an outline of the new play and was hoping to find someone to write the lines for her:

Je suis si maussade que je n'ai pas le pouvoir de travailler. Le plan de ma piece est pourtant fini. Je donnerois beaucoup a celui qui voudroit me la dialoguer. Je suis desolée qu'on m'ait demandé cette besogne. J'aurois eté si aise de passer mon eté sans rien faire. Mais il faut faire effort.[5]

She first turned to the abbé de Voisenon, whom she had known for years; they had been fellow members of mlle Quinault's 'Temple' in the early 1740s, had collaborated on the *Recueil de ces messieurs*, and had shared the triumphs of *Les Lettres d'une Péruvienne* and *Cénie*:

T'ai-je dit que j'ai fait le plan de ma piece pour Viene bien instructif et que la Merluche[6] me l'ecrira. Il ecrit tres bien les details. Cela sera bon pour cela. Il en est ravi car il n'ose plus travailler pour lui. On lui a fait jeter au feu trois comedie et des contes. Il ne croit pas en Dieu mais il a peur du diable. C'est une epate[7] pour lui que d'ecrire une comedie en sureté de conçience et moi je me gobergerai jusqu'au mois de septembre ou j'ai de grands desseins.[8]

Voisenon must not have been as overjoyed as mme de Graffigny believed; in any case, he refused. In despair, mme de Graffigny wrote to Devaux on 13 July:

Tiens, il faudra que je fasse mes Saturnales, je le vois bien, et j'en soufrirai surement. Ce petit vilain Enchois[9] m'a renvoyé mon plan; il n'y veut pas mordre. Je l'ai envoyé a Jean Jaques Rousseau qui est si malade que je suis sure qu'il me refusera. Je vais me tuer et cependant il le faut car je n'ai rien donné depuis qu'on m'a donné. On me demande. Ce seroit me donner un grand tort de ne rien faire. Je serai malade. Eh bien, j'aime mieux une maladie qu'un tort, apres avoir fait tout ce qui dependoit de moi pour l'eviter.[10]

[5] GP, lviii.271.
[6] pseudonym of the abbé de Voisenon (1708-1775).
[7] doubtful reading.
[8] mme de Graffigny to Devaux, 26 June 1752 (GP, lviii.288).
[9] pseudonym of Voisenon.
[10] GP, lviii.305.

Bret left an account of Rousseau's having written *Les Saturnales* in the same memoir quoted on his visits to the salon (Leigh, ii.310-13: appendice A81):

Une anecdote qui nous Regarde tous les deux trouvera naturellement sa place ici; Mad^e de Graffigny Etoit chargée depuis plusieurs années de la part de l'auguste Marie-Thérèze, mère de notre Reine actuellement régnante de lui Envoyer de petits drames dont cette impératrice qui veilloit de prez à l'Education de ses enfans leur distribuoit les Roles pour de secretes représentations qu'elle ordonnoit dans son palais.

Mad^e de Graffigny Etoit sujette alors à une incommodité peu ordinaire, Espèce de spasmes instantanés qui par la fréquence de ses retours, lui interdisoit tout Espèce de travail Et la privoit du talent qu'on lui connoissoit et dont elle avoit donné plus d'une preuve. Elle avoit déjà conçu l'idée du drame qu'on attendoit à Vienne, c'étoient *les Saturnales*, sujet heureusement choisi pour des princes qui dans ce canevas devoient voir ceux qui les servoient Elevés à leurs places tandis qu'ils Rempliroient les rôles subalternes: Mad^e de Graffigny s'étoit mise plusieurs fois à l'ouvrage Et reconnoissant trop qu'alors elle n'étoit plus Elle même, Et qu'elle alloit compromettre sa réputation, Elle se confessa au citoyen de Généve en le priant de la suppléer dans cette circonstance.

Mr Rousseau, auquel rien n'Etoit moins propre qu'un ouvrage de commande et qui étoit convaincu, comme il le dit, qu'il n'Eut jamais été lu s'il n'Eut écrit que pour Ecrire, se déffendit autant qu'il put mais il fut forcé de se Rendre aux sollicitations pressantes de la dame. On ne pouvoit lui laisser beaucoup de tems et il apporta ce drame qui à la vérité répondoit trop mal aux vues de l'auteur du sujet.

Mad^e de Graffigny En avoit senti la foiblesse et m'avoit prié de passer chez elle pour me raconter ingénument ce qui étoit arrivé. Elle me remit le Brouillon de Mr Rousseau et m'imposa au nom de l'amitié qui nous unissoit la dure loi de la mettre avant 6 jours en état de faire l'Envoi dont elle s'Etoit chargée.

La haute considération que m'avoit inspirée Mr Rousseau ne me permit aucune Réflexion jalouse relative à la préférence que lui avoit donnée mad^e de Graffigny sur un ami plus ancien: je me suis toujours déffendu d'Etre un fat, Et je n'Ecoutai que l'amitié qui réclamoit un service dont Elle (mad. de Gr.) avoit physiquement besoin dans ce moment.

Avec beaucoup de Zèle de l'Envie d'obliger une respectable amie (il faut bien que je le dise) je parvins à remplir le canevas dont m. Rousseau n'avoit point senti le mérite par la seule raison qu'il Etoit d'un autre que lui. Mad^e de Graffigny fut contente, on le fut à Vienne: Elle en Eut des preuves très convainquantes mais je ne crus pas pour cela En valoir mieux que le citoyen de Genève. . . .

J'ajouterai seulement que l'auteur des *Lettres de Zilia* et de *Cénie* me remercia hautement et devant un cercle fort nombreux, du prétendu service que je lui avois rendu, disoit elle, dans un moment ou elle Etoit infiniment pressée par le tems, Et où son incommodité qui duroit Encore, affaissoit son imagination au point qu'une lettre ordinaire Etoit pour elle une occupation qui redoubloit son mal Etre.

Once again, we must recognize that Bret's memory may have failed him in one or two details, but fundamentally his story is confirmed by mme de Graffigny's letters. It does not appear to be true, however, that she had to plead with Rousseau to accept the task, for he responded affirmatively to her first letter. She wrote to Devaux on 20 July:

Je viens de trouver en rentrant chez moi un billet qui m'aprend que Rousseau veut bien faire ma petite comedie. Cela me fait un plaisir qui efface presque l'autre[11] parce que je crai[n]s d'etre malade ou d'avoir un tort presque egalement.[12]

There followed some difficulties of a trivial sort; Rousseau was supposed to come to dinner on 23 July, and failed to appear. The party was re-scheduled for the next day, but the prince de Beauvau and the marquise de Boufflers signified their intention of coming by, and mme de Graffigny had to withdraw the invitation to Jean-Jacques. All this is described in a letter of 24 July:

[lundi 24 juillet 1752]

[Hier] Je devois avoir Jean Jaques Rousseau a diner. Je n'eus que la Plessi.[13] Cela est un peu different. Aujourd'huy il devoit venir, j'ai affaire a lui, et la Belle Dame[14] m'a mandé hier qu'elle viendroit manger de la tarte avec son frere[15] et le ⟨chevalier⟩ Vicomte.[16] Je viens de contremander Jean Jaques . . .[17]

Finally on 25 July, he came to dinner and they discussed the play. Despite its brevity, mme de Graffigny's relation of this conversation is fascinating:

[11] a bit of bad news she had just related.
[12] GP, lvii.17.
[13] pseudonym of a cousin of Léopold Desmarest, former lover of mme de Graffigny. Mme de Graffigny saw her often, and found her very tiresome.
[14] Marie-Françoise-Catherine de Beau-vau-Craon, marquise de Boufflers-Remiencourt (1711-1786).
[15] Marc-Juste de Beauvau-Craon (1720-1793).
[16] Louis-Auguste, vicomte de Rohan-Chabot (1721-1753).
[17] to Devaux (GP, lvii.21).

J'ai eu Jean Jaques a diner. C'est bien celui-la qui t'impatianteroit par ses visions cornuë. Je lui ai dit a diner qu'il s'etoit imortalisé en criant contre les arts, et que je voulois m'immortaliser en ecrivant l'histoire de ses folies. Il m'a offert des memoires. Il est tres aimable dans sa façon. Enfin nous avons raisonné de ma piece. Il ne vouloit pas ridiculiser Caton et je crois qu'il auras bien de la peine. Cependant nous sommes convenus de nos faits.[18]

If nothing else, mme de Graffigny had a keen sense of the timely subject. And if only she had known how the story of Rousseau's follies would one day immortalize Rousseau himself! It is tempting to speculate about the memoirs; but Rousseau was probably only joking, no doubt with more bitterness in his heart than he dared to let his hostess see. It is not even clear whether by follies mme de Graffigny meant his ideas, such as the attack on the arts, or things he had done.

The mention of Cato surely gives us the key to understanding why Rousseau consented to do this chore. The subject was to some extent in the air, thanks to Voltaire and Crébillon.[19] In their long rivalry, Crébillon had given a *Catilina* in 1748; he depicted Cato in an unfavourable light. Voltaire set to work the next year to compose his riposte, *Rome sauvée*, but used it mainly to distract attention from *Oreste*, which took aim at Crébillon's masterpiece, *Electre*, first acted in 1708 – in the middle of the eighteenth century, *Electre* had been performed at the Théâtre français more often than any of Voltaire's plays. *Rome sauvée* was put on in February 1752, and showed Cato from a much more favourable perspective. Mme de Graffigny had seen both plays, and ever alert for material for her playlets, she seized on the character Cato as a likely subject.

Rousseau's interest in Cato had deeper roots. In *Le Verger de madame de Warens*, published in 1739, he had written, 'Je m'exerce à marcher sur les pas de Caton' (*Œuvres*, ii.1124). Cato had been cited in the first *Discours*, and criticized bluntly by Charles Borde, who spoke of 'la folie de Caton: Avec l'humeur et les préjugés héréditaires dans sa famille, il déclama toute sa vie, combatit et mourut sans avoir rien fait d'utile pour sa patrie' (*Œuvres*, iii.87). Jean-Jacques retorted indignantly:

Je ne sçais s'il n'a rien fait pour sa Patrie; mais je sçais qu'il a beaucoup fait pour le genre humain, en lui donnant le spectacle et le modele de la vertu

[18] to Devaux, 25 July 1752 (GP, lviii.312).

[19] see Lancaster, *French tragedy in the time of Voltaire*, pp.333-60.

la plus pure qui ait jamais existé . . . Nos descendans apprendront un jour que dans ce siécle de sages et de Philosophes, le plus vertueux des hommes a été tourné en ridicule et traité de fou, pour n'avoir pas voulu souiller sa grande ame des crimes de ses contemporains, pour n'avoir pas voulu être un scélérat avec Cesar et les autres brigands de son tems.[20]

One can only marvel at the fact that, having read such lines, mme de Graffigny should propose to Rousseau that he write a play ridiculing Cato – and that Rousseau, having written such lines, should agree! His obsession with the character must have blinded him to what he was being asked to do.

Claude Pichois and René Pintard have just brought to light a small group of texts, written approximately at this time, in which Rousseau compares Cato to Socrates – indeed, the editors gave their book the title *Jean-Jacques entre Socrate et Caton.* As they point out, the rivalry between Voltaire and Crébillon was only the most visible aspect of an intellectual debate that went on throughout the first half of the century; Saint-Evremond, Bayle, Addison, Voltaire, Vauvenargues, Montesquieu, Prévost, all took part in it, and between 1749 and 1752 there were two important histories of the Catiline conspiracy, by Seran de La Tour and Bellet. Rousseau, one must imagine, was eager to have his own say, looking for a pretext to re-read the texts and to let his imagination dwell on this hero, in whom he so obviously was beginning to see his own reflection.

Mme de Graffigny was on the wrong side, though; she sympathized with Crébillon rather than Voltaire – and even Voltaire was far from the kind of veneration Rousseau professed – and with Borde rather than Rousseau. She conceived Cato as a Roman Misanthrope, inveighing fanatically against the impudence of his slaves, the coquetry of his sister Servilia, and the politics of Caesar. Nothing so momentous as a conspiracy plays any significant part in her plot, however; the conflicts are domestic and fundamentally comic. Rousseau was soon to revolutionize the world's opinion of Alceste, but in the French society of 1752, he and Cato were wrong to insist so rigidly on their excessively narrow morality.

Nor was the character of Cato the only area where there must have been conflict between Rousseau's convictions and mme de Graffigny's outline. The title, *Les Saturnales,* refers to a festival during which the

[20] *Œuvres*, iii.87-8.

usual rules of obedience, courtesy, and decorum were suspended, and all men were equal for a few hours. Here again, Rousseau may have been seduced by the idea in a broad sense; in the *Lettre à d'Alembert* and in *La Nouvelle Héloïse*, he analyzes the major importance of holidays and popular festivals in the political organization of society. Mme de Graffigny's ideas hardly accord with Rousseau's, however. For her, the Saturnalia were apparently an excellent institution, which gave the slave Dromon a chance to point out Cato's hypocrisy and vanity. It was also an occasion for lovers to meet, circumventing the austere proprieties of normal times. To judge by Rousseau's later statements, he must have agreed with Cato that no good could come of the promiscuous mingling of servants and masters, of flagrant violations of decorum, or of gross indulgences of the instincts.

Finally, the outcome of the plot simply reinforces the impression that Cato is wrong. Mme de Graffigny's outline called for him to be out-talked by the slaves, outwitted by Caesar, and ignored by everyone else. His only victory is in Servilia's humiliation; she thinks that Caesar loves her, but he is really using her only as a mask for his love of Cornelia, daughter of Cato's friend Sylla. In the end, Caesar, having taken advantage of the Saturnalia to sneak into Cato's house, makes gifts to Cornelia, spurns Servilia, defends himself against a false accusation of treason by Cato, and wins Sylla's consent for his marriage to Cornelia. It is perhaps worth recalling that the play was intended for an audience comprised of an emperor and his family and court. It is highly piquant to imagine Rousseau trying to dramatize his ideas for their edification.

Small wonder, then, that Jean-Jacques backed out in less than two weeks, as mme de Graffigny wrote to Devaux on 6 August. He had actually written only four pages, with a half-page margin and wide spaces between speeches. Mme de Graffigny preserved it, and it is reproduced in full in the following chapter. The story of the play is not yet complete, however; Bret, it will be recalled, thought that Rousseau had written a complete but unsatisfactory version. On this point, it was not, I think, his memory but his lady that deceived him. In the letter of 6 August, mme de Graffigny wrote as follows:

Jean Jaques est retombé malade et m'a renvoié mes paperasses. Je n'y avois pas beaucoup de regret car il a comencé et c'etoit le vray ton des pieces de colege. J'avois une ressource pour avoir plus d'une corde a mon arc. J'avois envoié mon plan au bonhomme Destouches. Il m'a renvoié hier la piece toute faite mais si plate, si bassement ecrite, si detestablement ecrite que je n'en puis garder un seul mot. Mais pas un. Me voila donc forcée de travailler et de travailler au quard d'heure. J'en suis desolée. Ah, je veux que tu voye cette besogne de Destouches, et la letre qu'il m'a ecrite afin que tu connoisse une bonne fois l'impertinente presomption des hommes. Malgré cela je ne lui suis pas moins obligée ⟨mais⟩ car il l'a fait de la melieure grace du monde. Mais je n'en enrage pas moins.[21]

Philippe Néricault Destouches was seventy-two years old when these events took place; he died two years later, and mme de Graffigny thought that he had lapsed into complete senility by then. He was in 1752 still one of the great playwrights of the century, most famous for *Le Glorieux* (1732), but a prolific author of new plays even in his seventies. Naturally, he was a member of the Academy. In short, he was a successful and highly respected figure, and mme de Graffigny could scarcely repay his favour, bungled though it had been, by allowing his poor work to be known publicly. Rousseau, on the other hand, was still known only for the first *Discours*, and was widely regarded as a crank. It is merely a guess, but I believe that mme de Graffigny must have told Bret that Rousseau had promised to help and had not given her what she wanted – that being of course true – and then passed on Destouches's manuscript, letting Bret draw the conclusion that it was Rousseau's. Bret was discreet, in any case; except for the memoirs he wrote in 1785, and never published, no other record of Rousseau's or anyone else's involvement has survived.

Bret also took more credit for his work than is really due him, although the honour of authorship is perhaps a dubious one. In a final letter, mme de Graffigny says that the final version is her own, and the manuscripts bear her out on the whole. She drew heavily on Bret's draft, but rewrote whole scenes herself. The complete play is given in the appendix, edited so as to show the parts that can be identified in the draft as being in mme de Graffigny's hand:

Je suis de bien bonne humeur aujourd'huy, mon ami. J'ai fini ce matin les Saturnales. On travaille a force a les copier. C'est un grand soulagement que le poids d'un pareil ouvrage hor de dessus les epaules [. . .]
Pardi tu sera las de Saturnales mais ce ne sera pas ma faute. Je t'envoye

---

[21] to Devaux (GP, lvii.39).

celle du Grand Garçon,[22] le comencement de celle de Jean Jaques et la miene. Le Metromane[23] l'a lue hier au soir; il en est tres contant. Je vais la porter a Nicole[24] et vite l'envoier. Ne prends pas garde a quelques mot repeté ou du meme son; nous les avons corrigé. C'etoit la premiere fois que je l'entendois lire et ce n'est jamais ⟨par la qu'on⟩ en ecrivant que l'on s'aperçoit de cela. Tu peux garder mon brouillon mais je te prie de me renvoier tous les autres des que tu les auras lu. Le Roi[25] part le dix; tu devrois tacher de me le faire tenir par quelqu'un de sa suitte. Je veux que tu me promette que tu liras celle de Bret la premiere; c'est mon modele, ainci il faut commencer par la.[26]

Both Bret and mme de Graffigny were deceived about the eventual reception of the play in Vienna. Prince Khevenhüller-Metsch recorded in his journal that it was performed on 28 October 1752, and mme de Graffigny soon received letters of praise and thanks, and more important to her, her pension. But the prince confided to his journal that their imperial majesties found the play too serious and the speeches too long, especially for the children. There, for all practical purposes, the history of *Les Saturnales* ended.

[22] pseudonym of Antoine Bret.
[23] the abbé Turgot.
[24] mlle Quinault *la cadette*.

[25] that is, Stanislas, who was coming from Lunéville to Versailles.
[26] mme de Graffigny to Devaux, 25, 26 August 1752 (GP, lviii.316, 318).

VI

Les Saturnales, fragment by Rousseau: text and commentary

Saturnales[1]

p^re bande d'Enfans.
Saturnales! Saturnales!

2e Bande d'Enfans
Saturnales, Saturnales!

prémier Enfant
Regarde un peu si nos maudits Pedans ne nous suivent point.

2e. Enfant
Grace au Ciel, la fête nous delivre d'eux, et ils n'auront d'aujourdui le plaisir de nous tourmenter

p^r. Enfant
Nous devrions bien profiter du[2] privilége des Saturnales pour leur rendre une partie des maux qu'ils nous font.

2e. Enfant
Comment pourrions nous nous venger d'eux?

p^r. Enfant
Allons leur chanter pouille en Grec.

3e. Enfant
Eh! non non. Tachons seulement de nous bien réjouir. C'est le – meilleur moyen de[3] les chagriner.

---

[1] GP, lxxxi.61-4. The text is arranged in two columns, the one on the left being intended for possible corrections and additions, according to Rousseau's habitual method (see Leigh ii.321-2: appendix A84). He abandoned the project quickly, however, and therefore added only one speech in the left-hand column. Thus, despite the small number of corrections, this is a first draft. The heading 'Saturnales' is written in pencil, by another hand.

[2] profiter ⟨de l'im⟩
[3] ⟨nous jouer⟩

p^r. *Enfant*

Tu as raison. Crevez, crevez, – maudits porte-tristesses. Saturnales!
Saturnales!

Tous crient à pleine tête.

Saturnales, Saturnales!

un Precepteur

Enfans ingrats! Pendant que vous ne songez qu'à vos plaisirs, c'est
le soin de vôtre bonheur qui nous occupe.[4]

Scéne 2.

Troupe d'Esclaves qui arrivent en dansant.

Un Esclave

Au plaisir qui s'apprête
Livrons-nous en ce jour
Nous pouvons, grace à la fête
Etre foux à nôtre tour.
Le Chœur répéte ces 4 Vers.

L'Esclave

Rompons d'indignes entraves
Bravons nos[5] Tyrans jaloux.
Si le sort les eut fait esclaves
Ils vaudroient encor moins que nous.

Un Esclave

Doucement, Messieurs, nous fesons[6] un Vacarme de tous les Diables,
sans songer que c'est ici la Maison de Caton.

Dromon

N'admirez-vous pas la simplicité de celui-ci; il est si accoutumé aux
coups d'écourgée qu'il les croit prets à fondre sur lui.

---

[4] this speech is written in the left-hand
column.
[5] ⟨non [?]⟩
[6] ⟨vous faites⟩

l'Esclave

Point; je n'ignore pas les priviléges que la fête nous donne. Et c'est moins la crainte que le respect qui me fait parler.

Dromon

Ah! oui; du respect pour ce radotteur éternel! ne voudrois-tu point respecter aussi la vieille coquette de sœur, qui est assés folle pour croire Cesar amoureux d'elle?

L'Esclave

Non, je t'abandonne Servilia avec tous ses ridicules; Mais pour Caton je soutiens que tout le monde doit des hommages à sa vertu. Ah! c'est un Romain celui-là.

Dromon

Ma foi, c'est à mon avis une très médiocre louange,[7] et je le dispenserois volontiers d'être si Romain s'il vouloit être un peu plus homme.

un 3ᵉ Esclave

Tu en parles avec bien de l'aigreur. J'augure un peu qu'il te traitte mal.

Dromon

Non; c'est le plus doux de tous les maitres. Et la moitié des bons traittemens qu'il fait à ses gens suffiroit pour l'en faire adorer, s'il savoit y joindre cette douceur qui fait valoir tout le reste.[8] Mais sa morgue Romaine me desespére. Je le hais - parce qu'il me méprise. J'aimerois cent fois mieux qu'il me fit moins de bien et qu'il me témoignât plus de considération.

1ʳ Esclave

Ah! Ciel; le voila lui-même; sauvons nous tous.

Les Esclaves, s'enfuyant

Sauvons nous tous

---

[7] louange ⟨que celle là⟩
[8] qui ⟨les⟩ fait valoir.

Dromon

L'imbecille effroi[9] de tous ces[10] sots là me réjoüit. L'aspect d'un Romain est pour ces ames serviles[11] comme celui des Dieux pour les ames superstitieuses; un objet[12] de terreur plustôt que de respect. Pour moi je me suis aguerri en voyant de près celui ci.[13] Sa vertu m'en impose moins depuis que j'ai connu[14] qu'elle n'est qu'une vertu de parade. J'en aimerois[15] mieux une moins orgueilleuse et plus permanente, que l'on portat partout avec soi.

Even in these few words, one can detect Rousseau's originality straining against the limitations of mme de Graffigny's banal outline. All the versions begin with expository scenes using a group of pupils and a group of slaves, but only Rousseau brings in the preceptor, and sketches the motives for a teacher-student antagonism. We are a long way from *Emile*, and mme de Graffigny is correct to describe this as 'le vrai ton des pièces de collège'. To criticize the traditional education as pedantic, to admit that the children suffered under it, were not new ideas. In fact, mme de Graffigny herself had expressed similar ideas about women's education, with more style and sophistication, in her *Lettres d'une Péruvienne*. Yet it is Rousseau alone who allows the children to speak for themselves, and the point deserves to be noted. At the same time, he allows the preceptor a line in his own defence, a pompous platitude to be sure, yet its sober moral tone reflects Rousseau's real feelings. If this preceptor is an ancestor of Emile's governor, he is too distant to trace the genealogy. What is striking, however, is the operation of Rousseau's mind on the materials given him; he develops a dynamic relationship, in which ambiguous characters embody complex ideas, whereas mme de Graffigny wanted a schematic situation, clearly defined characters, and simple ideas.

With the slaves, Rousseau extends the same technique of deepening and complicating mme de Graffigny's idea. The attack on slavery, the argument that servitude created vices, were again not original, at least in such rudimentary form. These sentiments are consistent with the *Contrat social*, but would not lead anyone to predict that their author

---

[9] Rousseau hesitated over this word, and crossed out heavily those he rejected: ⟨terreur⟩ ⟨effroi⟩

[10] ⟨ses⟩

[11] serviles ⟨?⟩

[12] objet ⟨de⟩

[13] voyant ⟨celui ci⟩ de près.

[14] ⟨senti⟩

[15] ⟨voudrois⟩

would some day write the *Contrat social*. Instead, Rousseau displays his genius in endowing the slaves with the capacity to make subtle moral distinctions, and in establishing a dynamic relationship between them and their masters. The slave who speaks in defence of Cato foreshadows the servants at Clarens, in his susceptibility to good example, and in his sense of respect which lies deeper than the urge to misbehave. He is a servant formed by Julie's principles, with all the humility and timidity that implies. His fearful flight at Cato's appearance marks him as a slave, and Rousseau never thought that men could have the virtues of citizens and those of slaves at the same time.

Dromon, who was destined by mme de Graffigny to play a traditional *valet fourbe* role, becomes a spokesman for Rousseau himself in some regards. He is superior to his station, as Rousseau himself had been when he was in service. In his first speech, he shows himself capable of transcending his social definition, and understanding the difference between the virtues of slaves and those of masters. He has a difficult position to defend, however, for Cato cannot be sacrificed to justify the slaves' resentment. Dromon first attempts to divert the argument, by mentioning Servilia. This is obviously necessary for the exposition, but serves to refine the other slave's position: he is not servile before all the ruling class, only respectful before those who have earned it.

This tactic having been thwarted, Dromon is put on the defensive by the statement that Cato is a true Roman, and he parries by drawing a distinction between Roman and human. Rousseau may have had in mind a reminiscence of the famous line from *Tartuffe*: 'Ah! pour être dévot, je n'en suis pas moins homme' (iii.iii), in which case Dromon is hinting at hypocrisy and impugning Cato's integrity. A third slave presses the attack on Dromon, charging that he is speaking out of personal bitterness. This provides the pretext for one of the most interesting speeches in this fragment, as Dromon tries to explain why it is that he hates Cato.

Cato is, in fact, a benevolent and gentle master, who treats his slaves well. What Dromon cannot stand is his contempt. Dromon would gladly give up the charity in exchange for more consideration, as he calls it; he wants equality. This is certainly Rousseau's authentic voice, not only recalling the days of his youth when he smarted under the gaze of those he served, but also repeating the declaration of personal independence he was then making. Within a few months, he would decline a pension from the king himself; he had already determined to earn his living through the honest work of music copying he was contemplating resigning from a lucrative job with Dupin de not through the humiliating favours of the great. At about this time Francueil, from the same motives. Dromon's speech is thus a cry from Rousseau's heart, attenuated by the limitations of mme de Graffigny's plot.

In the final speech of Rousseau's fragment, Dromon makes explicit his earlier hint that Cato was a hypocrite. Dromon, having discovered this, has lost all his fear and respect. As a bit of moral and social analysis, the transmission of vices from masters to servants is obviously in harmony with Rousseau's theory of the contagion of virtues. The spread of vice, indeed, was a readily observable fact, according to contemporary opinion, and thus a more common idea.

In terms of the development of the play, however, Rousseau has encountered an obstacle, and it may well have discouraged him from struggling to continue. The relationship implied between Dromon and Cato could be developed into a very interesting work of literature; in a sense, many of Rousseau's works do develop it. Within the constraints of mme de Graffigny's plot, however, Rousseau could not proceed as he needed to. For her purposes, Cato had to have some serious fault, and in the final version, he has many. What Dromon calls his 'morgue romaine' would surely not suffice; but that leaves Rousseau at an impasse. To make Cato a hypocrite is a false start; hypocrisy is not consistent with the feelings Dromon expressed in the previous speech. Almost any other flaw would make his high reputation implausible. In short, the only way Rousseau would consent to weaken the character of Cato was far too subtle for the needs of the story, and probably for the possibilities of the genre, and maybe even for Rousseau's talent. For one of the most unsatisfying elements in his mature works is the character of the master: Wolmar, Emile's governor, the Legislator are too idealized; they are indeed too perfect and not human enough. Even in these four pages, it must have become obvious to Rousseau that the ideas he had about Cato, about education, about festivals, and about equality, which had induced him to undertake this work, could never in fact be developed in it. Consequently, on the pretext of his genuinely poor health, he abandoned it.

VII

Rousseau and mme de Graffigny after Les Saturnales

Mme de Graffigny's letters contain nothing to suggest that she ever saw Rousseau in person again, after their abortive collaboration on *Les Saturnales*. The letters are not conclusive proof, however. We have seen already that Rousseau is hardly mentioned in the spring of 1752, although other sources document his presence at mme de Graffigny's salon. Even under ordinary circumstances, then, he might not have been mentioned and yet have been a frequent guest. After the summer of 1752, however, circumstances seldom favoured mme de Graffigny's sending a full record of her activities to Devaux. Some of the reasons can easily be guessed. As a prominent hostess, mme de Graffigny had less time to write and more to write about. As she grew older, her always poor health got worse The principal causes for the increasing irregularity of their correspondence, however, were accidental and unpredictable.

In the autumn of 1752, two of Devaux's long-cherished dreams were realized: his play, a one-act comedy called *Les Engagements indiscrets*, was staged by the Théâtre français; and he was made a member of the academy of Lorraine. That academy had been founded only a few years before, under the patronage of king Stanislas. Devaux, naturally, knew all the members and had been much involved in the preliminary discussions. He was mortified, however, not to have been a charter member; and indeed, his feeble qualifications were openly disparaged by some whom he had supposed to be supporters. The acceptance of his play by the Théâtre français – his first real publication – must have helped open the doors to him. He then had, of course, to write a *discours de réception*. His ego had always been tender when anyone criticized his writing, and mme de Graffigny knew it; but he regularly sent her his works, and she criticized them, and every few months they replayed the scene of Alceste and Orgon's sonnet. This time it became more serious, because it was for the public, and it coincided with the unfortunate results of the play.

That the play was put on at all, Devaux owed to mme de Graffigny's patience and persistence. When she came to Paris in 1739, she had in her baggage the manuscript of a play by Devaux, and one of her first enterprises was to have it produced. Throughout the 1740s that effort never entirely ceased. The text was sent back for revisions, the actors stalled, or the author sulked about some obstacle. The final version probably bore no resemblance to the manuscript of 1739. Predictably, the play was poorly received, and was withdrawn after four performances. Its chances were not improved when the leading actress, la Lamotte, fell on her derrière at the première. But even a flop, to reach the public, required influence and industry, all of which had come from mme de Graffigny. The nervous Panpan felt so anxious about the waiting that he asked mme de Graffigny to keep her labours a secret from him, a request she honoured, so that she announced the performance as a surprise, in a letter of 24 October 1752.[1]

Far from being grateful, as soon as he learned what had happened, Devaux blamed her for his humiliation and took to his bed. Mme de Graffigny accused him of hypochondria, and that angered him still more. Petty as all this is, it had the effect of displacing most of the other subjects from the correspondence. Surely she heard some rumours about the success of *Le Devin du village* at Fontainebleau on 18 October, and Rousseau's departure the next day, which apparently shocked his friends enough to create a stir; but that was in the midst of the final preparations for *Les Engagements indiscrets*.

The quarrel over the play ended by mid-winter, but the pattern lasted until mme de Graffigny's death ended the correspondence. A single topic would tend to dominate their discussion, which usually degenerated into a dispute. For example, in the spring of 1753 they argued over Fréron's admission to the academy of Lorraine; that summer, over Devaux's laziness; in the spring of 1755, over Devaux's health; in the late autumn and winter of 1755 and 1756, over Devaux's decision to spend the winter in Lunéville; in the summer of 1756, over a sinecure that mme de Graffigny was trying to arrange for Devaux. In 1753 and in 1756, the quarrels actually led to a temporary halt of several weeks in their exchange of letters.

Finally, the largest gaps in the correspondence were caused by Devaux's trips to Paris. He had come to Paris for the winter of 1733-1734, and made one trip to see mme de Graffigny in 1747-1748; but

---

[1] 24 October 1752 (GP, lvii.162); 27 October 1752 (GP, lvii.163); 5 November 1752; (GP, lvii.175-8).

he refused all mme de Graffigny's other invitations on the grounds that he had to stay with his aged parents. His father died in 1753, and his mother in February 1754; that August, he came to Paris with the marquise de Boufflers, and stayed in the area until March 1755. He returned for a short time in November 1755. He came once again in 1756, probably around September; the correspondence had already been interrupted by a quarrel, but they patched it up in person, and the flow of letters resumed again with Devaux's return to Lunéville in April 1757. And finally, he came in August 1757 and stayed until May 1758.

In short, for the six years preceding mme de Graffigny's death, her correspondence with Devaux was totally interrupted for more than a third of the time; and even when they were regularly sending letters, they often became obsessed with personal matters. The letters are therefore only a partial guide to mme de Graffigny's activities, and to the literary gossip of Paris during that period. Despite these limitations, Rousseau is named from time to time, generally because of some publication or well-known incident.

Rousseau's name reappeared first in connection with the presentation of his play, *Narcisse, ou l'amant de lui-même*. Rousseau had written this play years before and never succeeded in having it performed. The actor La Noue, no doubt encouraged by the success of the first *Discours*, and then of *Le Devin du village* at Fontainebleau, induced his colleagues at the Théâtre français to put it on for the first time on 18 December 1752. The play itself has always attracted less attention than the incidents surrounding it. Jean-Jacques himself tells how, after the first performance, he went across the street to the Café Procope and declared himself to be the author and confessed that he found the play bad: 'Pour moi, je m'ennuyai tellement à la prémiére que je ne pus tenir jusqu'à la fin, et sortant du spectacle, j'entrai au caffé de Procope où je trouvai Boissi et quelques autres, qui probablement s'étoient ennuyés comme moi. Là je dis hautement mon *peccavi*, m'avouant humblement ou fierement l'auteur de la Piéce, et en parlant comme tout le monde en pensoit' (*Confessions, Œuvres*, i.387-88). Mme de Graffigny's story is much like Rousseau's:[2]

De crainte de n'avoir pas trop de tems demain, je profite d'un petit

[2] mme de Graffigny to Devaux, 19-20 December 1752 (GP, lvii.251-3).

moment pour te dire qu'une petite piece donnée hier est tombée. Cela est tout simple. Mais ce qui ne l'est pas, c'est ceci. Depuis trois semenes qu'on parle de cette piece tout le monde crioit a tue tete qu'elle etoit de Jeanjaques Rousseau et moi je criois plus fort qu'elle n'en etoit pas, parce que je n'accordois pas cela avec son caractere feroce, et que sachant que Duclos lui avoit arraché son opera, je n'ymaginois pas qu'il se voulout de plain gré faire sifler sur le theatre françois. Mille autres chose me tenoit ferme dans mon opinion. Elle estoit pourtant fausse car la piece est de lui. Elle se nomme L'Amant de lui-meme. Voici ce que c'est en deux mot. C'est un fat dont une femme veut se moquer. Elle le fait peindre en habit de femme et lui fait rendre se portrait misterieusement. Il ne se recconnois pas et devient amoureux de lui meme. On dit que cela est mal fait, mal ecrit, plat et maussade. Je soutenois encore hier a tout le monde qu'elle n'etoit pas de lui. Je le croiois encore a midi et a une heure le Grand Garcon[3] qui est venu diner avec moi m'a detrompée en me contant que Rousseau en sortant de sa chute etoit entré chez Procope, qu'il avoit demandé les nouvelles, qu'on lui en avoit dit quelqu'unes. Il dit, 'Je vais vous en dire une plus fraiche, Mrs, c'est que la piece qui vient de tomber est de moi. Si elle avoit eu du succes je ne le dirois pas.' On a voulu dire qu'elle n'avoit point eté eccoutée et qu'elle etoit mal jugé. 'Non, Mrs, on a entendu et l'on a bien jugé.' Esse de la folie ou de l'heroisme. Cela fait voir que l'un et l'autre se touche car on a peine a les demeler. J'avois compté y aller mais les pars ne se sont point arrangé. [. . .]

On dit que La Noue a travaillé depuis hier a rapetasser L'Amant de lui meme et qu'on la donnera demain. J'yrai et je t'en dirai encore de plus sures nouvelles. [. . .]

J'arrive de Merope qui m'a fait un grand plaisir, et la piece de Jean Jaques aussi mais [? ce n'est] pas ce que vous pensez. C'est que j'avois dans ma loge le Petit, le Metromane, le Vicomte, et le Beau P . . .[4] Ces deux derniers n'ont cessé de dire, 'Il n'y a pas de comparaison de Jean Jaques a Panpan. Celui la est une piece, celui ci est un chifon;' Enfin le pauvre Jean Jaques a eté fort mal traité et toi fort loué, et tout le monde a raison. D'abord ce n'est pas une piece. Et cependant il y a deux intrigues sur lesquelles on pouroit dire, 'Jean danse mieux que Piere, Piere danse mieux que Jean.' Les entrés et les sortiees sont frequentes mais il n'y a que dieu qui sache pourquoi. La manchette en homme et en femme est effleurée partout. Enfin c'est une pitié. On ne s'en prendra pas aux acteurs car la Grandval y fait merveille et la Gaussin pas mal. Les hommes sont Drouin et Bellecourt.[5]

[3] pseudonym of Antoine Bret.
[4] pseudonyms of Saint-Lambert, Turgot, the vicomte de Rohan-Chabot and the prince de Beauvau.
[5] see Rousseau, Œuvres, ii.957n.

This letter suggests that mme de Graffigny had not seen Rousseau for some time; she was well informed about *Le Devin du village*, no doubt by Duclos, but her opinion on *Narcisse* was simply guesswork. Of course, Rousseau himself would not have betrayed the secret, which he thought at the time only Gauffecourt, d'Holbach, Grimm, Mussard, and La Noue knew (Leigh 187), although he concedes in the *Confessions* that many others had got wind of it. Mme de Graffigny, though, would surely have said something about his slyness if he had personally misinformed her about his authorship. Bret's account of the incident in the Café Procope differs slightly from the version in Clément and La Porte's *Anecdotes dramatiques* (Leigh 188, note *b*), but all accounts agree on the essential points.[6] It is not clear from mme de Graffigny's letter whether Bret himself was among those present in the café, or whether he merely heard the story later. In any case, it was a fresh rumour at the time.

La Noue very likely did try to salvage the play; he had sponsored it and made the arrangements to have it staged anonymously. He was, furthermore, an author himself. On the same day mme de Graffigny was writing to Panpan, Rousseau wrote to La Noue to inform him that the author's name was public, and to release La Noue from any further obligations (Leigh 188).

Rousseau's play had been put on with Lefranc de Pompignan's *Titon* the first night; mme de Graffigny saw the second and last performance, when it was accompanied by Voltaire's *Mérope*. Her judgement of the play is very harsh, but she turns the incident into a compliment to Devaux, whose self-esteem was still smarting. Mme de Graffigny's company in the theatre, Saint-Lambert, Turgot, the prince de Beauvau, and the vicomte de Rohan-Chabot were among her closest friends. All except Turgot were from Lorraine, and thus friends of Devaux too. Even Turgot professed admiration for Panpan's poetry, according to mme de Graffigny; but as his pseudonym suggests, he was a fanatical lover of verse at the time.

Mme de Graffigny's succinct criticism of the play's double plot seems to reflect the general appraisal. Rousseau appreciated the acting less enthusiastically than mme de Graffigny, but granted that 'on ne

---

[6] Pierre Clément and Joseph de La Porte, *Anecdotes dramatiques* (Paris 1775), i.48.

pouvoit pas appeller cela une Piéce absolument mal jouée' (*Confessions, Œuvres*, i.387). On one point, her impression deserves to be noted: the homosexual implications of the play, with its transvestite disguises and coquettish fop, did not escape contemporary audiences. Jacques Scherer has commented on these hints of sexual deviance, but apparently underestimated the freedom of the theatre at the time, or the sophistication of the spectators (*Œuvres*, ii.1863-64). A few days later mme de Graffigny noted, 'L'Amant de lui meme a fini mercredi'.[7]

If anything, the publication of the play surpassed the staging in scandal, because of the preface Rousseau attached to it. In the *Confessions*, he remembers it with pride: 'Cependant, comme il étoit sûr que la piéce, quoique glacée à la réprésentation, soutenoit la lecture, je la fis imprimer, et dans la Préface, qui est un de mes bons écrits, je commençai de mettre à découvert mes principes un peu plus que je n'avois fait jusqu'alors' (*Confessions, Œuvres*, i.388). Readers and critics like Grimm and Fréron thought otherwise, but all focused their attention on the preface. Mme de Graffigny was no exception; announcing that she had sent him a copy, she called Devaux's attention to the preface: 'Je me rejouis de voir ce que vous direz de la piece de Rousseau que je vous envoyai avant hier, et surtout de la preface.'[8]

Three days later she gave her own judgement:

Je pourois bien n'etre qu'un sot, mais que dis-tu de la prefasse de Rousseau? Je lui conseille encore de nous chanter injure apres nous avoir donné une si mauvaise piece. Pour le coup j'en abbandonne le parti. Ses orgueilleux haillons me revoltent et je crois que Gormas,[9] son grand brailleur, n'en fait guere moins. Je lui demandai il y a quelque jour ce qu'il en disoit. 'Ma foi,' dit-il, 'ce sont les petites maisons ouverte, c'est tout ce que je puis dire.' Tu[10] sais qu'il est copiste, ce Rousseau. Il y a quelque jours que le Comte de Clermont[11] lui fit copier quelque chose et lui envoia 25 louis que l'autre renvoia apres avoir pris son dus. [. . .][12]

This was a sort of game between them; to play within the rules, Devaux had to read the work and pronounce his judgement before receiving mme de Graffigny's. The fun, of course, was to induce

[7] 23 December 1752 (GP, lvii.258).
[8] 16 February 1753 (GP, lix.72).
[9] pseudonym of Duclos
[10] ⟨sais⟩ tu
[11] Louis de Bourbon-Condé, comte de

Clermont (1709-1771), 'prince du sang', academician in 1754.
[12] to Devaux, 19 February 1753 (GP, lix.75).

Devaux to say he liked something that everyone else disliked, or vice versa.

Mme de Graffigny claimed at least to have been one of Rousseau's admirers up to this point, despite her disagreement with the thesis of his *Discours* and her negative judgement of *Narcisse* on the stage. Her disaffection here must be measured against some later events, too; she was won back almost immediately by *Le Devin du village*. Duclos's alleged comment is interesting, for he remained one of Rousseau's friends after most of the others had fallen under suspicion. Mme de Graffigny cannot entirely be trusted in such matters, however; she had a normal propensity to badger conversational partners into agreeing with her. Duclos must have found his life in society somewhat difficult at this time, however, for Rousseau's reputation for eccentricity and rudeness was growing, and Duclos was widely known to be his friend and sponsor.

The anecdote concerning the comte de Clermont would seem to be the earliest appearance of a story that recurs in various forms. In December 1757 or January 1758, Deleyre heard the story and repeated it to Rousseau, as follows: 'Mais je ris beaucoup, l'autre jour, d'entendre dire que vous aviés refusé cent loüis de Mr. le prince de Clermont, tandis que vous ne payiés pas votre blanchisseuse. Je suis sûr que vous n'auriés pas eu moins de plaisir que moi. Ce qu'il y a de singulier, c'est que le prince eut peut etre été dans le cas de vous faire cette générosité aux dépends de quelque créancier. Car voilà comme va la monde, et celle qui vous envoya les cinquante loüis auroit beaucoup mieux fait de ne les avoir pas volés au peuple. Cependant, n'en aiés point de remords, il vous etoient dus à cent titres' (Leigh 597).

Except for the inflation, to be expected after five years, Deleyre's tale is a close echo of mme de Graffigny's. Not long before, the same Deleyre had relayed to Rousseau the rumour, attributed explicitly to mme de Graffigny, that he had broken off with Diderot during, and because of, the latter's difficulties with the *Encyclopédie* and *Le Fils naturel* in August 1757 (Leigh 518). Deleyre may well have been among those who frequented her salon, and thus could have picked up the tale directly from her; or, obviously, he could have heard it from one of her guests. The allusion to 'celle qui vous envoya les cinquante loüis', that is, to mme de Pompadour, suggests a date for the incident: March 1753; for there exist two versions of a letter from Rousseau on

7 March, accepting fifty *louis* from the marquise with evident hesitation and discomfort. Moreover, one of the manuscripts is annotated as follows: 'Mr de Gauffecourt ami particulier de Rousseau m'a raconté qu'il s'etoit trouvé par hazard chés cet homme celebre au moment ou l'un des valets de chambre de mde de Pompadour etoit venu luy apporter ces 50 loüis en y joignant les expressions les plus flatteuses d'estime et de bonté de la part de sa maitresse: cet homme singulier avoit d'abord refusé opiniâtrement le present qu'il n'accepta que vaincu par les remontrances et les importunités de son amy qui eut encore bien de la peine a l'engager d'ecrire ces quatre lignes de remerciments a sa bien faitrice' (Leigh 195bis, notes critiques). Finally, an anonymous *gazetier* of the period described the incident very much as Gauffecourt did in an entry dated 30 March; Leigh concludes plausibly that Gauffecourt must have circulated some version of the story very soon after the event. The same *nouvelliste* alluded also to the comte de Clermont, but in relation to another subject: the dedication and *avertissement* to the text of *Le Devin du village*. The anecdote is related as follows: 'On a parlé devant le Roi de cet avertissement impertinent, et sa Majesté dit: S'il me plaisoit aussi d'envoyer le S. Rousseau à Bicêtre, et de l'y faire fustiger, ajouta M. le Comte de Clermont' (Leigh app.92.a).

It is hard to know how much credence to give these tales. The marquise de Pompadour's gift, if not Rousseau's recalcitrance, is certainly a fact; but it happened in March, after her own performances in *Le Devin* on 4 and 6 March, or perhaps still later after the publication of the text (but see mme de Graffigny's letter of 4 March). Mme de Graffigny's story cannot be an embroidery on that incident. It is consistent with Rousseau's character, especially his new resolve to live independently, that he should have rebuffed the comte de Clermont; and the *gazetier*'s association of Clermont's name with the king's angry reaction to the foreword strongly suggests some sort of incident between him and Rousseau. Indeed, Clermont's aristocratic advice to the king is much more comprehensible if he had himself suffered personally from Jean-Jacques's impertinent independence.

Twelve days after sending the book, mme de Graffigny had Devaux's reply, and she noted with satisfaction that they agreed on the preface to *Narcisse*:

Certe voiez. La preface de Jean Jaques est la plus impertinente chose du monde. Le Petit[13] dit un bon mot sur lui ici il y a deux ou trois jours. On en parloit et des 25 louis du Comte de Clermont renvoyé. Le Petit dit, 'Il faut convenir qu'il n'y eut jamais un gueux si jaloux de sa besace.' Je ne sais rien de plus expressif et qui peigne mieux ce vilain cinique que je ne puis plus soufrir. On donne demain son opera ici. J'irai vendredi a la seconde representation. Je trouve que Marivaux dit fort bien. 'On devient donc homme singulier quand on veut,' dit-il, 'car j'ai connu ving ans Jean Jaques et il ne l'etoit point du tout.'[14]

The rest of the passage shows that the rumour about Clermont had been spread among her circle, at least; Saint-Lambert is not, however, a likely source for Deleyre's report in 1757, because he was with the army at the time. Marivaux's witticism must be slightly misquoted; he had known Rousseau for about ten years, not twenty. Rousseau saw him regularly in 1742, and says in the *Confessions*, 'Je montrai même [à Marivaux] ma Comedie de *Narcisse*. Elle lui plut, et il eut la complaisance de la retoucher' (*Confessions*, *Œuvres*, i.287). He had more reason than most to be astonished at the evolution of Rousseau's mind, and to smile at certain passages from the preface to *Narcisse*: 'J'ai écrit cette Comédie à l'âge de dix-huit ans, et je me suis gardé de le montrer, aussi long-tems que j'ai tenu quelque compte de la réputation d'Auteur' (*Œuvres*, ii.959).

As the preceding letter announces, the scandal over *Narcisse* was soon to be overshadowed by the talk about *Le Devin du village*, which opened in Paris on 1 March 1753. Since it had been staged at Fontainebleau in the autumn, with great success, it was eagerly awaited by the Parisians, including mme de Graffigny:

Je crains d'etre si fatiguée tantot que je ne puisse t'ecrire, mon ami. Je dine chez Nicole[15] et je vais a l'opera. C'est bien de la besogne pour quelqu'un qui etoit morte hier au soir pour avoir diné chez la Vielle Comtesse[16] sans panier et fort a mon aise. Je suis d'une foiblesse inimaginable. Cependant j'ai une telle envie de voir l'opera de Rousseau que je passe par dessus tout, quitte pour me jeter au lit en rentrant. [. . .]
J'arive de l'opera moins malade que je ne l'aurai cru. Je suis enchantée de l'opera de Rousseau. Celui de Collé[17] n'a pas pris a cause du baragoin des acteurs qui prononcent le françois comme de l'arrabe.[18]

---

[13] pseudonym of Saint-Lambert.
[14] 28 February 1753 (GP, lix.86).
[15] pseudonym of mlle Quinault *la cadette*.
[16] pseudonym of the countess of

Sandwich.
[17] *Le Jaloux corrigé*, an *opéra bouffon* in one act by Charles Collé.
[18] mme de Graffigny to Devaux, 2 March 1753 (GP, lix.87, 89).

The opera went a long way toward rehabilitating Rousseau in mme de Graffigny's esteem, but the scandal of the dedication and preface burst on the public immediately: 'Je t'ai fait copier l'avertissement que Jean Jaques a mis a la tete de son opera et sa dedicasse a Gormas.[19] Si tu veux les parolles, tu les auras.'[20] It would appear from this letter that the printed text was available a few days sooner than has been supposed, and mme de Pompadour might have sent the fifty-louis gratification for a copy as well as for a performance, as early as 7 March 1753 (see Leigh 195bis, notes expl.).

Mme de Graffigny liked the opera well enough to see it a second time, and it continued to be talked about:

Je vais a l'opera ce soir dans la loge du Marquis de Stainville[21] et avec lui.[22]

Je vais seulement repondre a un article qui me fait rire et que tu as raison d'apeller rabachage. Tu croiois aller a l'Aurore de Rousseau et tu n'as trouvé que celui de Montcrif et de Rebelle.[23] Vois si cela n'est pas risible. La piece de Jean Jaques ne s'apelle point l'Aurore mais le Devin du vilage, et en verité l'aurore n'y le crepuscule n'y ont rien a voir.[24]

Mr. Orgon[25] ne reprendra pas. Collée m'a donné une bonne scene ce matin de sots qui sont ne se doute pas d'eux meme. Je savois qu'il faisoit un vacarme horrible dans Paris contre J. Jaques parce qu'il ne lui a pas rendu une visite de remerciment pour les couplets dont le refrain est 'C'est un enfant' qu'il lui a donné. Il m'a reccommencé ses plaintes ameres, vehementes sur cette impolitesse dont il fait un crime atroce, sans se doutter le moins du monde que c'est le succes du Devin et la chute d'Orgon qui le mettent en colere. Ah, que cela est bon pour le spectateur. [. . .]

Oui, c'est au Devin du vilage que je suis retourné[e] et qui m'a fait le meme plaisir, mais ce n'est pa[s] le fils Stainville[26] qui m'a preté sa loge. Il a bien d'autres besogne. C'est le pere, grosse bete.[27]

In a note to his second *Dialogue*, Rousseau admits three trivial borrowings for *Le Devin*, including 'Les paroles de la chanson qui

---

[19] pseudonym of Duclos; see Rousseau, *Œuvres*, ii.1093-94 and *n*.

[20] mme de Graffigny to Devaux, 4 March 1753 (GP, lix.91).

[21] François-Joseph de Choiseul, marquis de Stainville; see the letter of 13 March, which follows.

[22] mme de Graffigny to Devaux, 9 March 1753 (GP, lix.99).

[23] mme de Graffigny wonders elsewhere in this letter whether Devaux was

thinking of *Titon et l'Aurore* by Mondonville, first presented on 9 January 1753.

[24] mme de Graffigny to Devaux, 11 March 1753 (GP, lix.101-102).

[25] character in the *Jaloux corrigé*.

[26] the son is Etienne-François, duc de Choiseul, future minister of foreign affairs. On the father, see the letter of 9 March, above.

[27] mme de Graffigny to Devaux, 13 March 1753 (GP, lix. 106-107).

sont, en partie, et du moins l'idée et le refrein de M. Collé' (*Œuvres*, i.870). The song in question is a 'vaudeville' of six stanzas, which comes near the end of the opera (*Œuvres*, ii.1111-13). Collé's *Le Jaloux corrigé* had opened on the same day as *Le Devin*, but passed quickly into oblivion, as mme de Graffigny wrote on 2 March. Her estimation of Collé's claim agrees with Rousseau's own feeling that attacks on his musical ability, and rumours of his plagiarisms, had been products of jealousy. Collé, however, did not belong to the same coterie as Grimm, Diderot, and d'Holbach, the friends Rousseau thought betrayed him; and there is virtually no other trace of any contacts between him and Rousseau. We can observe here, and in the Clermont incident, the early stages of two phenomena: the spread of false accusations and slanders about Rousseau; and his confusion of real threats and malicious attacks with the tactless but mostly well-meant pressures of his friends.

By this time, Rousseau's reputation as a madman was well established; mme de Graffigny sent the following epigramme to Devaux on 6 May:[28]

> Trois auteurs que Rousseau l'on nomme
> Sont distinguez; voici par ou:
> Rousseau de Paris fut grand homme,
> Rousseau de Geneve est un fou,
> Rousseau de Toulouze un atome.

One should not infer that mme de Graffigny endorsed the thought. The next time Rousseau appears in the letters, she is scheming with Duclos to have him become an academician:

> A propos, j'ai toujours oublié de te dire un complot que nous avons fait et dans lequel tu peut tout faire. C'est de faire nommer Jean Jaques Rousseau de l'Accademie de Lorraine. Gormas[29] se charge de le faire accepter. Le Roi n'y doit avoir nule repugnance car il l'a loué plus delicatement qu'il ne l'a jamais eté dans sa replique,[30] et ce seroit une bonne contrediction a tous ces ecris que de le voir dans une accademie. Ameute tes dames pour cela, je t'en prie, aupres du Roi et du Chancelier.[31] Tu me fera un grand plaisir.[32]

---

[28] 6 May 1753 (GP, lix.191).
[29] pseudonym of Duclos.
[30] in his reply to Stanislas' refutation of the first *Discours*.

[31] Chaumont de La Galaizière, chancellor of Lorraine.
[32] mme de Graffigny to Devaux, 30 May 1753 (GP, lix.226).

The plan, one must note, was not lacking in mischief, and mme de Graffigny was no doubt motivated in part by a wish for revenge; for Rousseau had ended the preface to *Narcisse* with an explosion of contempt for normal social behaviour, including these lines:

S'ils s'aperçoivent jamais que je commence à briguer les suffrages du public, ou que [. . .] j'aspire à des places d'Académie, ou que j'aille faire ma cour aux dames qui donnent le ton, ou que j'encense la sotise des Grands [. . .] je les prie de m'en avertir, et même publiquement, et je leur promets de jetter à l'instant au feu mes Ecrits et mes Livres, et de convenir de toutes les erreurs qu'il leur plaira de me reprocher.[33]

Duclos's role is ambiguous – typical of the general attitude of the time, but unexpected from the one man who kept Rousseau's trust to the very end. He had, as mme de Graffigny reported earlier, torn Rousseau's opera away from him to get it presented. Plainly, he had powers of persuasion over Rousseau that no one else possessed. Moreover, by everyone's testimony, notably mme d'Epinay's, he was an inveterate meddler in the affairs of others, presumably with the best of intentions. Having arrived in the social and literary world to a position of great power, by the most traditional routes, he very likely thought that membership in an academy would serve Rousseau's interest. The subject was apparently broached with Rousseau, who mentions in the *Confessions* having 'refusé à M. de Tressan et en quelque sorte au Roi de Pologne d'entrer dans l'Academie de Nancy' (*Œuvres*, i.520); and so the plan came to nothing.

Devaux in any case refused to co-operate, apparently on the grounds that Rousseau had insulted the abbé Gautier in replying to his refutation of the first *Discours*:

Ah, pour le coup, rien ne manque a ta façon de penser a gauche, puisque tu trouve plus honnete d'avoir acuilly Freron[34] que de faire Rousseau de l'Accademie. L'un est un honnete homme et l'autre un mechant homme. Jean Jaques a ploté ton sot d'abbé Gautier[35] qui l'avoit attaqué directement. L'autre est un chien enragé qui mort tout le monde. Tiens, quand on prend le change en toute rencontre sur les sentimens et qu'il faut avoir recours pour etre entendus a des distinction theologique pour les deffendre, il n'y a pas moien de s'accorder avec les gens qui n'ont que la droite raison et le

[33] *Œuvres*, ii.973-4.
[34] Fréron was named to the Académie de Nancy on 8 May 1753.
[35] Gautier had refuted the first *Discours*; Rousseau replied with his *Lettre à Grimm* (*Œuvres*, iii.59-70).

bonsens pour guide. Eh bien, n'en parlons plus. D'autres n'auront pas de si puerilles et de si fausses considerations.[36]

Fréron's nomination to the academy had taken place earlier in the spring, and had already provoked a great deal of sarcasm from mme de Graffigny; she brought him up here only for the comparison. She had good reason to regard Gautier as a fool; in 1750 he had sent her a manuscript entitled *Réfutation du Celse moderne*, which was a defence of orthodox Christianity against one of the clandestine criticisms then circulating. In order to reply, however, Gautier first had to publish the criticisms, and by universal agreement readers in Paris found the criticisms much more convincing than Gautier's replies. It was only through personal appeals to Malesherbes that mme de Graffigny had been able to recover the dangerous manuscript from the censors in order to return it to the abbé, who then published it in Lorraine. We should bear in mind also that Devaux had quarrelled with mme de Graffigny about his own admission to that academy. Her annoyance here stemmed from private grievances against Devaux, more than from her admiration for Rousseau.

From this moment on, references to Rousseau become less and less frequent. The correspondence was slow during the summer of 1753, because of a dispute. On 8 July, there was an allusion to Rousseau's letter in the *Mercure*, regarding the dangers of using copper utensils (Leigh 200): 'L'article de Jean Jaques m'a bien divertie aussi bien que toi.'[37] On 5 August, mme de Graffigny explained a mix-up in sending books to Devaux, who had wanted Borde's second refutation of the first *Discours*, called *Second discours sur les avantages des sciences et des arts*:

J'ai ri de bon cœur et fort fachée cependant de vous avoir envoyé l'impertinent Discours sur les ars et les sciences.[38] C'est une betise de Duchéne[39] qui me l'avoit aporté au moment de la poste pour celui de Mr de Borde.[40] Quand le lendemain je voulu le lire je connus l'erreur et je ris de ce que vous croiriez que c'etoit un mauvais tour. Il faut en gratifier l'Exelence.[41] Je vous envoye aujourdhuy le veritable dont je suis enchantée. Voila ce qui s'apelle

[36] mme de Graffigny to Devaux, 6 June 1753 (GP, lix.236-7).
[37] 8 July 1753 (GP, lix.290).
[38] that is, Rousseau's *Discours*.
[39] Parisian book-dealer, mme de Graffigny's publisher since 1752.
[40] see *Œuvres*, iii.103n.
[41] Chaumont de Lucé, brother of the chancellor of Lorraine, diplomat; Devaux had the job of ordering books for his library.

penser et raisonner. Je ne crois pas que Jean Jaques y reponde.[42] Je veux absolument connoitre cet esprit sage et éloquent.[43]

Jean-Jacques had mentioned this work in a letter written to its author in May 1753; it was published during the summer of 1753. It is true that Rousseau did not reply, but mme de Graffigny was probably expressing her opinion that Borde had had the last word, not revealing any news she heard from Rousseau himself. She had, it will be recalled, advised him not to reply to Borde's first refutation.

In the autumn of 1753, the bad feelings between Devaux and mme de Graffigny interrupted their letters for a time. Starting again in 1754, mme de Graffigny sent Devaux a copy of Fréron's *Lettres sur quelques écrits de ce temps* with this comment: 'Je t'envoye aussi les Feuilles. Le morceau contre Jean Jaques est de Bret.'[44]

The piece referred to is an anonymous letter to Rousseau, hesitantly attributed heretofore to Ozy or Fréron, which was published in Fréron's *Lettres* in January 1754.[45] It was one of the numerous ephemeral works produced by the famous *Querelle des Bouffons*. The Bouffons were an Italian troupe, who arrived in Paris in August 1752, and performed on the opera stage. Their presence brought into the open a debate between partisans of French music, including Rameau and most of the established musicians of the royal academy, and those of Italian music, including most of the Encyclopedists. Grimm made his reputation with a pamphlet, *Le Petit prophète de Boemischbroda*, in January 1753, favouring the Italians. Rousseau, who nursed a long-standing grudge against Rameau, and who was the *Encyclopédie*'s resident authority on music, brought forth his *Lettre sur la musique française* in November 1753. It was one of the last major incidents, but certainly one of the most violent.

Since Bret was a close friend of mme de Graffigny's, there is no reason to doubt her attribution of the letter to him. Bret's tactic was to trap Rousseau in the contradiction between his condemnation of the arts on the one hand, and his proposals to improve French music on the other. At about this same moment, Montucla was writing to the academy of Lyons: 'On n'a vu pendant assez longtemps que paraître de jour à autre des écrits contre [Rousseau], presque tous pitoyable

[42] he began a letter but abandoned it; see *Œuvres*, iii.103-107.
[43] GP, lix.320.
[44] 14 January 1754 (GP, lxi.8).
[45] see Denise Launay, ed., *La Querelle des Bouffons* (Genève 1973).

[. . .]' (Leigh 209). Whether or not he counted Bret's contribution among them, it is certain that Bret's innocuous rhetoric was among the least of Rousseau's concerns at the time.

Rousseau introduces the story in the *Confessions* by remarking: 'La description de l'incroyable effet de cette brochure seroit digne de la plume de Tacite' (*Œuvres*, i.384). Montucla, d'Argenson, Grimm, and others confirm the intensity of the storm precipitated by Rousseau's *Lettre*. Palissot wrote to Jacob Vernes on 18 December: 'La lettre de J. J. Rousseau lui a fait une foule d'ennemis, on l'a pendu en effigie à l'orquestre de l'opéra, il y'a eû une Lettre de cachet expédiée contre lui pour le Renvoier à Genève [. . .]' (Leigh 205). D'Hémery's *gazetier* related many of the same details, and reported on 19 December: 'Dimanche dernier, Rousseau s'etant présenté à la porte de l'opera pour y entrer, l'homme qui est à la porte lui dit qu'il n'avoit plus ses entrées' (Leigh, app.92.i).

Rousseau himself devotes a long passage to this last incident:

La Ville venoit d'avoir la direction de l'Opera. Le prémier exploit du Prevot des Marchands fut de me faire ôter mes entrées, et cela de la façon la plus malhonnête qu'il fut possible; c'est à dire, en me les faisant refuser publiquement à mon passage; de sorte que je fus obligé de prendre un billet d'amphithéâtre pour n'avoir pas l'affront de m'en retourner ce jour-là. L'injustice étoit d'autant plus criante que le seul prix que j'avois mis à ma piéce en la leur cédant étoit mes entrées à perpétuité: car quoique ce fut un droit pour tous les Auteurs, et que j'eusse ce droit à double titre, je ne laissai pas de le stipuler expressement en présence de M. Duclos [. . .] Il y avoit dans ce procédé une telle complication d'iniquité et de brutalité, que le public, alors dans sa plus grande animosité contre moi, ne laissa pas d'en être unanimement choqué, et tel qui m'avoit insulté la veille crioit le lendemain tout haut dans la salle qu'il étoit honteux d'ôter ainsi les entrées à un Auteur qui les avoit si bien méritées et qui pouvoit même les réclamer pour deux. Tant est juste le proverbe Italien qu'ogn'un ama la giustizia in casa d'altrui.

Je n'avois là-dessus qu'un parti à prendre; c'étoit de réclamer mon ouvrage, puisqu'on m'en ôtoit le prix convenu. J'écrivis pour cet effet à M. d'Argenson qui avoit le département de l'Opera, et je joignis à ma lettre un Mémoire qui étoit sans réplique, et qui demeura sans réponse et sans effet ainsi que ma lettre.[46]

[46] *Confessions, Œuvres*, i.385.

Mme de Graffigny mentioned the incident briefly:

Ils sont chassés enfin, ces Bouffons, et on a auté les entrées a l'opera a Jean Jaque, ce qui lui donne presque raison, tant la vangeance est basse et injuste. Il est vray que pour un balet d'un acte on n'a qu'un an les entrée, mais il a fait la musique et les parolles, de droit il a deux ans.[47]

The most interesting aspect of the letter is its date. The Bouffons were sent away on 7 March 1754, victims of the pro-French cabal. But why was it still newsworthy that Rousseau had lost his right to free entry into the theatre four months earlier? If there was a shift in public opinion, as she and Rousseau both asserted, would it not have occurred much sooner? Moreover, mme de Graffigny was not alone in sending the news in March; Charles-Georges Le Roy mentioned it in a letter to Pierre-Michel Hennin on 15 March (Leigh 216). Perhaps the reason was that Rousseau's appeal to d'Argenson did not take place until March; the letter he wrote is dated 6 March (Leigh 214, 214bis) and may have revived a furor that had died down.

That leaves unexplained, however, why Rousseau waited so long. All the evidence indicates that the crowd's greatest hostility to him came in December 1753, right after his *Lettre* appeared; it was then that he was jostled, threatened, and insulted. Thus he concurs with the *gazetier* in placing his exclusion from the theatre in December, yet he writes as if his appeal to d'Argenson were an immediate response. More astonishing still, he places the incident right after the transfer of authority for the Opera to the city of Paris – which had occurred in August 1749.[48] Obviously, as Rousseau wrote the *Confessions*, there were some confusions about dates; furthermore, there was another misunderstanding about the *entrées*. If perpetual free entry to the theatre were a right for all authors, why should he have taken the trouble to stipulate it? In fact, writing to Saint-Florentin in 1759 on this same topic, Rousseau recognized the existence of a time-limit on the *entrées*, but claimed that it had been invented expressly to exclude him (Leigh 214, note c). Mme de Graffigny's comments suffice to prove the falsity of that charge; at the same time they show the legitimacy of Rousseau's grievance. Much of the confusion, no doubt, arose from the fact that the *entrées* were controlled apparently by

[47] to Devaux, 19 March 1754 (GP, lix.68-9).
[48] see J. B. Durey de Noinville, *Histoire* *du théâtre de l'Académie royale de musique en France*, second edition (Paris 1757); reprint (Genève 1972), p.102.

custom, not official policy; the royal regulations forbade any free entries except to an author's own works.[49]

The likeliest explanation for these inconsistent facts is that the exclusion in December was the work of an individual, or possibly several, supported by the mob's fury against Rousseau; but they were not carrying out any policy nor any orders from the prévot des marchands. In the weeks following, Rousseau undoubtedly continued to be mistreated at the opera house, and perhaps went on buying his ticket to avoid confronting the man at the door again; on 1 March 1754, his year of free entry expired, and at that point the loss of the *entrées* was official policy, no doubt jubilantly enforced and published by the opera staff; then Rousseau, his paranoia understandably flaring, felt that a plot had been formed against him, wrote to d'Argenson, and concluded that injustice had triumphed when his appeal failed. In recalling the events for the *Confessions*, he associated his being barred at the door in December – a flagrant injustice – with the loss of his *entrées* in March – possibly a normal procedure.

Mme de Graffigny's letters provide no further help on the matter, and in the summer of 1754, Devaux came to Paris so that the correspondence ceased for several months. Rousseau meanwhile had departed for Geneva, and was composing his second *Discours*. Upon Devaux's return to Lorraine in 1755, with the resumption of their correspondence, mme de Graffigny wrote twice about early rumours of the *Discours sur les origines de l'inégalité*:

Vraiment oui, je sais du nouveau: les Matines de Cithere,[50] un livre de Jean Jaques sur l'egalité des condition. J'ai fais batre les libraires sans avoir pu les trouver. Ce sera pour l'ordinaire prochain.[51]

Je ne t'envoye aucun livre. Celui de Rousseau s'imprime en Hollande. Il n'est pas fini et l'on ne sait encore si l'on obtiendra la permission de le faire passer.[52]

Her informant was knowledgeable, and may have been Malesherbes himself, who was in fact at that very moment considering whether or not to grant permission for the book to be sold in France. Marc-Michel Rey had sent him the main part of the book in late March; Malesherbes acknowledged it 2 April. Rey forwarded the last pages on 24 April.

[49] Durey de Noinville, p.116.
[50] *La Nuit et le moment, ou les matines de Cythère* (1753) by Crebillon *fils*.
[51] 23 April 1755 (GP, lxii.39).
[52] 26 April 1755 (GP, lxii.197).

83

On 12 May, Malesherbes gave permission for one hundred copies, but Rey sent fifteen hundred, begging that he be allowed to put them on sale right away to prevent pirated editions from capturing his market. Apparently this was allowed, and the work was available in early June.[53]

The single copy Malesherbes had was enough to spark the rumours, however. By 5 May, they had come back to Rousseau, who wrote and asked Malesherbes to return the copy to him (Leigh 293) and on 29 May he wrote in annoyance to Rey, 'A la suite de tout cela, il est arrivé comme je l'avois prévu, que l'exemplaire que vous aviez envoyé à M. de Malesherbes a couru Paris, le bruit en est venu jusqu'à Genéve, on y est persuadé que l'ouvrage paroit ici et l'on s'indigne avec raison qu'il soit offert aux étrangers avant ceux à qui il est dédié' (Leigh 297). What mme de Graffigny may have thought of the *Discours* when it appeared is not related in the letters; she and Devaux were feuding again in the summer of 1755, and he made a brief trip to Paris in the autumn.

During that winter, Lorraine became the scene of an incident involving Rousseau. Palissot, a native of Lorraine, who had been one of mme de Graffigny's protégés in 1750 and 1751, wrote a play called *Le Cercle, ou les originaux*, in which Jean-Jacques and others were satirized. The play was performed on 26 November 1755, as part of a ceremony to dedicate a new statue of king Stanislas. On 15 December, the comte de Tressan, one of the founders of the academy of Nancy, wrote to king Stanislas, probably at d'Alembert's instigation, attacking Palissot and demanding that he be punished (Leigh 346). Devaux, a friend of Tressan's, Palissot's, and fellow member of the academy, naturally had intimate knowledge of the affair; but he and mme de Graffigny were still on guard with each other, and he withheld whatever he knew, drawing this rebuke:

Mon Dieu, que tu es bien Mr. Je. Tu dis mille vetilles qui te regardent, pas un mot du train que fait la comedie de Palissot,[54] de la letre de Mr de Tressan au Roi[55] et de tous ces trains la. Je t'ai bien reabilité dans l'esprit de Duclos en lui montrant comme tu a pris le parti de Jean Jaques.[56]

---

[53] see Rousseau, *Œuvres*, iii.1860-61, and Leigh 269-302 *passim*.
[54] *Le Cercle, ou les originaux*.
[55] Leigh 346.
[56] 19 December 1753 (GP, lix.318-19).

It is difficult, under the circumstances, to know how to read the final sentence; it was probably sarcastic. Devaux's role in the affair was in any case insignificant.

About a month later, mme de Graffigny wrote to Devaux:

> J'ai vu la letre de Jean Jaques avec une du pere Leslie[57] qui l'envoye a Boissi[58] pour le Mercure prochain. C'est le plus plaisant contraste du bon esprit avec le faux, de l'eloquence avec l'enflure que j'aye vu de ma vie.[59]

Rousseau's letter, dated 29 November 1755, was printed in the January *Mercure*; it was itself a response to a letter to the *Mercure* from 'un Bordelais', printed in the same number; and the whole series goes back to Voltaire's famous letter of thanks to Rousseau for his copy of the second *Discours*, which appeared in the *Mercure* in September 1755. Leslie was another member of the group of scholars and men of letters in Nancy; no letter to Rousseau has ever been attributed to him, but mme de Graffigny's description would fit one which appeared in the *Mercure* of March 1756, dated 14 January and signed 'un bourgeois de Bordeaux'. Leslie was obviously not from Bordeaux, but might have adopted the signature because of the previous letter. The editor of the *Mercure*, Boissy, was a regular guest and close friend of mme de Graffigny's; he may very well have shown her the manuscript and confided the author's name to her. Her opinion of it must once again be evaluated with her grudge against Devaux and his academy in mind.

For the rest of 1756 and 1757, Devaux was in Paris more than in Lorraine; there are long gaps in the correspondence, and no mention of Rousseau for a full year. In August 1757, when Deleyre heard mme de Graffigny's remark about Rousseau's break with Diderot, Devaux was in Paris. In 1758, however, just three months before her death, mme de Graffigny had the satisfaction of reading Rousseau's flattering footnote about her in the *Lettre à d'Alembert*. By this time she was dictating most of her letters, and the allusions are brief and mostly practical:

'Que dis-tu de Rousseau?'[60]

---

[57] Ernest Leslie (1713-1779), priest attached to the court of Lorraine.

[58] Louis de Boissy (1694-1758), playwright, had been director of the *Mercure* since 1754.

[59] 14 January 1756 (GP, lxiv.1-2).

[60] 12 September 1758 (GP, lxvi.101).

'Il y a dans le paquet que Messieurs Rainsaut te remettront un Lettre de Jean Jacques pour Monsieur de Lucé.'[61]

'Je t'envoye encore La Porte a cause de Jean Jaques qui me semble bien mené.'[62]

'Tu aura encore cette fois cy la feuille de La Porte. Je voulois la renvoyer mais comme elle traitte de la Lettre de Jean Jacques, et qu'elle est traitté joliment, je l'ay gardé, et tu m'en saura gré.'[63]

'Je n'y trouve qu'un defaut, c'est le prix. Il coute 4^{11} 4s, et la Lettre de Rousseau 3^{11} 12. Il faut avouer que ces Mrs vendent cher leurs coquilles.'[64]

Mme de Graffigny died on 12 December 1758; her health had been so bad for several months that she no longer went out, and her circle was limited to her closest friends. Her mind remained alert, nonetheless, and she was rereading Marivaux at the time of her death, with renewed pleasure. The fatal attack of her chronic illness came during a game of cavagnol with the abbé de La Galaizière, Du May, and Saint-Lambert, three men who had been steady, loyal friends from before the time she left Lorraine. On 8 December, she wrote that she knew the end was near, but was awaiting it without fear.

If Rousseau was aware of her death, he left no record of it. He had, or thought he had, good reason to complain of her treatment of him, notably her gossip about his break with Diderot. Even in 1751 and 1752, though, they had little in common; she neither understood nor accepted his ideas, and treated him as a successful and influential woman would a struggling neophyte, teasing, wheedling favours, offering officious help. The extent of the intellectual gulf between them must have become clear to Jean-Jacques in his brief fling at writing her *Saturnales*. Diderot was surely right when he wrote of *La Lettre à d'Alembert* in his *Tablettes*, 'Il y fait l'éloge de m^{de} de Grafigni qu'il n'estime ni comme femme de lettres ni comme femme' (Leigh, app.206); but Diderot was just as surely wrong to include that truth in a list of Rousseau's alleged 'scélératesses'. It was, on his part,

---

[61] 13 October 1758, dictated letter (GP, lxiv.105). Messieurs Rainsaut operated a courrier service between Paris and Lorraine. On Lucé, see note 41 on p.79, above.
[62] 27 October 1758 (GP, lxvi.125); La Porte was the author of a literary periodical, *L'Observateur littéraire*. Rousseau's *Lettre* was reviewed in letter vii (20 October 1758), pp.145-70.
[63] 30 October 1758, dictated letter (GP, lxvi.128).
[64] 2 November 1758 (GP, lxvi.133); the first book referred to is the *Discours sur la poésie dramatique* by Diderot.

86

a generous and compassionate gesture, all the more if it violated his professed allegiance to the truth and absolute sincerity.

VIII

The plotting of book viii of the Confessions

The years when mme de Graffigny was writing about Rousseau correspond almost exactly to book viii of the *Confessions*, which tells the story of his reform, from the illumination of Vincennes to early 1756, just before the move to the Hermitage. It is obviously a crucial time in the evolution of Rousseau's thought and the progress of his career, yet one of the least known. As Claude Pichois and René Pintard comment, 'Les *Confessions* sont, au sujet de cette période, imprécises ou d'une clarté inquiétante. Les lettres qui nous en sont parvenues sont rares et parfois trompeuses. . . .'[1]

The time is now past, surely, when Rousseau's veracity or mendacity were matters of passionate and often political concern; nonetheless, in his case biography takes on a significance it has for few other great figures. The ideas that Rousseau began to formulate and express around 1750 concern his life, and the individual lives of his readers, in a unique and revolutionary way. Even the first *Discours*, which Rousseau himself disparaged later, arose from a sense of personal alienation from society. In the preface to *Narcisse* in 1753 he wrote, 'Il faut, malgré ma répugnance, que je parle de moi' (*Œuvres*, ii.959). We may smile a bit at the parenthetical phrase, but the sentence is the first shot in a literary revolution; from that date on, the writer's self has never ceased to be the topic of central interest. To speak of one's self, and to denounce the division of the self into a natural and a social being, lead naturally to a problem of moral philosophy, that of sincerity. Rousseau demanded that his veracity be a subject of critical concern. Otherwise, his system would have been no more than another *philosophes'* paradox.

Ultimately, then, in spite of his repugnance, he was forced to write not just about, but *exclusively* about himself. Few people have ever so fully transformed their lives into a literary text. Yet as Georges May observes, for the reader this may be an obstacle as much as a help: 'Retrouver la continuité vivante de l'existence d'un homme n'est

---

[1] *Jean-Jacques entre Socrate et Caton,* p.108.

jamais chose aisée. Dans le cas de Rousseau, l'entreprise est rendue plus difficile encore par le soin même qu'il prit de nous la faciliter.'[2] The text is not the life, but a special representation of the life. 'C'est un portrait métamor . . . non, métaphor . . . oui, métaphorisé', babbles the drunken valet in *Narcisse* (*Œuvres*, ii.1006), and we may as well use Rousseau's pun in our own context. Rousseau's autobiographical literature, especially the *Confessions*, is a metaphor for the man himself; at the day of judgement he will point to the book and say, 'Voila ce que j'ai fait, ce que j'ai pensé, ce que je fus' (*Œuvres*, i.5). In the world, it will be 'le seul portrait d'homme, peint exactement d'après nature et dans toute sa vérité' and 'le seul monument sûr de mon caractère qui n'ait pas été défiguré par mes ennemis' (i.3). As a metaphor, it has its own value; one need not do research on Rousseau's life and times in order to read the *Confessions*. But these works are at the same time metamorphoses of a life, and it can only enrich our reading of the metaphor to discover by what metamorphosis it was created.

Book viii is troubling not only for its obscurity and silences about Rousseau's life, but also for its lack of inner coherence and pattern. The Pléiade editors write: 'La narration de ce livre VIII se morcelle, ce qui se voit aussi ailleurs, mais ce défaut de continuité n'est pas compensé ici, comme c'est le cas souvent, par le prolongement d'une note fondamentale ou par un contrepoint opposant deux ou trois registres affectifs' (*Œuvres*, i.1425). To some degree, this discontinuity reflects a simple chronological structure. Accidents and the intrusions of outsiders impinged on the smooth direct thrust of Rousseau's own internal progress, and he complained of it. Yet there are departures from a calendar chronology, the most notable being the discussion of the *Lettre sur la musique française* published in November 1753, before any mention of the failure of *Narcisse*, which occurred in December 1752. There are others, and still more events that Rousseau told in such a way as to avoid giving any date. This is not to over-emphasize the importance of dates; they matter only to the extent that Rousseau's transpositions reveal his interpretations of events.

Rousseau justified himself in advance regarding the truthfulness of his account. By his standards, mistakes in dating cannot be cited as proofs of lying or hypocrisy, only as honest and indeed irrelevant

[2] Georges May, *Rousseau par lui-même* (Paris 1961), p.5.

slips of memory. Introducing the second half of the *Confessions* Rousseau addressed the question as frankly and bluntly as possible: 'Ma premiére partie a été toute écrite de mémoire et j'y ai dû faire beaucoup d'erreurs. Forcé d'écrire la seconde de mémoire aussi, j'y en ferai probablement beaucoup davantage' (*Œuvres*, i.277). He did not claim to offer a true history of the events, but of his own soul (*Œuvres*, i. 278):

Tous les papiers que j'avois rassemblés pour suppléer à ma mémoire et me guider dans cette enterprise, passés en d'autres mains ne rentreront plus dans les miennes. Je n'ai qu'un guide fidelle sur lequel je puisse compter; c'est la chaîne des sentimens qui ont marqué la succession de mon être, et par eux celle des évenemens qui en ont été la cause ou l'effet [. . .] Je puis faire des omissions dans les faits, des transpositions, des erreurs de dates; mais je ne puis me tromper sur ce que j'ai senti, ni sur ce que mes sentimens m'ont fait faire; et voila dequoi principalement il s'agit. L'objet propre de mes confessions est de faire connoitre exactement mon interieur dans toutes les situations de ma vie. C'est l'histoire de mon ame que j'ai promise, et pour l'écrire fidellement je n'ai pas besoin d'autres mémoires: il me suffit, comme j'ai fait jusqu'ici, de rentrer au dedans de moi.

The passage is justly famous, and has often served to define Rousseau's purposes; but it is worth remarking that Rousseau would have *preferred* to use the documents. He relied on memory alone because he had no choice. He minimized as much as he could the errors he might make: omissions, transpositions, errors in dates (is that a complete list, or just an illustrative sample?), and he justified as best he could the method he was forced to use. This argument implicitly recognizes that readers will be bothered by the mistakes, and also implies Rousseau's intention to remain as close to documentary truth as circumstances allow. Given pure freedom to follow his feelings, he would no doubt have produced a far more structured account than he actually did.

We are left with the explanation – and how plausible it is! – that Rousseau's inner life was in such confusion from 1749 to 1756, that he simply could not make sense of it. Before and after, he could distinguish clear and uniform blocks of time: 'ma paisible jeunesse' or 'mes beaux ans passés avec autant de tranquillité que d'innocence' (*Œuvres*, i.277), followed by 'l'abyme de maux où je suis submergé' (i.589). The period of transition must have appeared to him as it does to us, full of contradictions, uneven, erratic, incoherent. On the one hand, the illumination of Vincennes and the unfolding of Rousseau's system revealed to him his own and his society's corruption, and he reformed his life. On the other hand, he wrote an opera and staged a play, he engaged in extended polemical battles over his first *Discours* and then over Italian music, he began to move widely in Parisian society, and finally he decided to compete for another prize with another discourse. One could hardly illustrate better a writer's typical pattern of success in the mid-eighteenth century, yet this was the man who had written to Voltaire in 1750, 'J'ai renoncé à la littérature' (Leigh 149). From the moral point of view, he did something still worse, sending three more of his children to the orphanage.

It is easy, then, to make the case that the tension, which runs throughout the *Confessions*, between a reality full of inconsistencies and a willed unity of structure, broke apart in book viii because of the impossible strains of the facts. At the very least, something of this sort must have worked to prevent the composition of one of the orderly books such as he wrote in the first half. There remains, however, the fact that one way or another Rousseau had to organize his narration of this period. Such facts as he recalled, or chose to relate, such feelings as belonged to the period, or could be attributed to it, had to be put into words. By looking carefully at this metamorphosis, as best we can determine it from the documents we now have and the text Rousseau has provided us, I think we can perceive a plan that, in a sense, represents Rousseau's understanding of his reform. This plan had to be subtle and complex, since Rousseau knew as well as anyone else what disparate material he had to account for. As a plan, it therefore lacks the mythic grace of the pastoral books of his youth, and also the obsessive plot structure of the paranoid books to follow.

As Rousseau presents book viii, it was obviously a time of unhappiness. The very first line reads, 'J'ai dû faire une pause à la fin du précédent livre. Avec celui-ci commence dans sa prémiére origine la longue chaine de mes malheurs' (i.349). It is true that Rousseau tended to see the origins of his unhappiness everywhere, from the moment of his birth onward; but that repetition and exaggeration does not alter the tone he meant to give book viii.

Posterity has elected the illumination of Vincennes as the key moment of this book, perhaps of the *Confessions*, of Rousseau's life, indeed of eighteenth-century thought. The incident occurs at the start of book viii, and has been deliberately de-emphasized by Rousseau, who claimed not to be able to remember the details, since he had written them down in a letter to Malesherbes. The letter to Malesherbes demonstrates that this had been a genuine mystical illumination for Rousseau; but in the *Confessions*, all he retains of that dramatic experience is the unhappiness it brought him: '[Diderot] m'exhorta de donner l'essor à mes idées et de concourir au prix. Je le fis, et dès cet instant je fus perdu. Tout le reste de ma vie et de mes malheurs fut l'effet inévitable de cet instant d'égarement' (i.351). Of the composition of the *Discours*, he says only that he conceived his ideas at night and dictated them to madame Le Vasseur in the morning. And the finished work he judges harshly: 'cet ouvrage, plain de chaleur et de force, manque absolument de logique et d'ordre; de tous ceux qui sont sortis de ma plume c'est le plus foible de raisonnement et le plus pauvre de nombre et d'harmonie' (i.352).

The illumination of Vincennes is actually treated by Rousseau as just one of a series of events in the larger event of the first *Discours*, and he has further reduced its impact by interspersing digressions between the incidents. After the inspiration and composition, he tells of his friendship with Grimm and Klupfell, and the shameful evening the three of them spent with Klupfell's mistress. Only then does he return to the *Discours*, deprecatingly: 'L'année suivante 1750, comme je ne songeois plus à mon discours, j'appris qu'il avoit remporté le prix à Dijon' (i.356). This reawakened his enthusiasm briefly, but he digresses again, this time to tell the story of his illegitimate children, his relations with the Dupin family, and finally his ill health. It was on his sickbed that he learned of the great success of his discourse, which Diderot had had published for him. Paradoxically, Rousseau says less about this incident than the previous ones, and attributes less role to himself; yet its effect on him was greater: 'Cette faveur du public nullement briguée et pour un Auteur inconnu, me donna la prémiére assurance véritable de mon talent dont malgré le sentiment interne j'avois toujours douté jusqu'alors' (i.363). This effect was, nonetheless, social and psychological, not intellectual; Rousseau concluded that being famous he could now earn his living copying music, and set about reforming some of his ways of living. The section on the first *Discours* does not end, however, until he has been lionized by the

Parisian salon society, and become entangled in the polemics over his *Discours*. As the section concludes, he observes: 'Voila comment les désagrémens imprévus d'un état de mon choix me jettérent par diversion tout à fait dans la litterature, et voila comment je portai dans tous mes prémiers ouvrages la bile et l'humeur qui m'en faisoient occuper' (i.368).

The fragmentation of this narrative is not accidental, nor is it an effort to deceive us; it is a rhetorical device for de-emphasizing the illumination of Vincennes and the first *Discours*. In the intervals between the moments of conception, of winning the prize, of publication, Rousseau has accumulated the shameful and unhappy facts of this period, with an occasional wrench of the chronology. In relating his connections with the Dupins, Rousseau puts his tenure as cashier, and his resignation for the post, in 1750-1751; but R. A. Leigh has shown that it must have been in 1752. Similarly, he abandons his children in the narration before January 1751, although the fifth child must have been born at least a couple of years later. One could scarcely argue that he had concealed these events; at worst he has re-arranged the dates. Yet the result of this transposition has not been to make him seem a better man, but rather, I think, to group several morally related incidents together. The year of his first *Discours*, from late 1749 until the first days of 1751, was an almost uniformly bad year. Rousseau became ensnared in treacherous friendships, immoral activities, economic bondage, intellectual prostitution – and the first *Discours* blended into, in fact went far to create, that ugly tonality.

Despite his rhetoric of sudden revelations and dramatic turning points, Rousseau does not claim to have changed his life from one instant to the next, nor even to have remained wholeheartedly committed to a reform from a moment early in the process. Writing about the news that he had won the prize, he says: 'Quoique la mauvaise honte et la crainte des sifflets m'empêchassent de me conduire d'abord sur ces principes et de rompre brusquement en visiére aux maximes de mon siécle, j'en eus dès lors la volonté décidée, et je ne tardai à l'executer qu'autant de temps qu'il en falloit aux contradictions pour l'irriter et la rendre triomphante' (i.356). This first phase of the reform was primarily a passive one. Inspiration and the news of his successes came to him when he least expected it. He was urged to compete by Diderot, and Diderot handled the chore of publication for him. His first reactions were fatigue and illness. Even when his will was set on reform, he still required the goad of contradiction to turn idea into act. Moreover, as the *Confessions* tell it, the first impulse of the reform was personal, not intellectual or literary; whence his impression (i.362) that:

Ce fut moins ma célébrité litteraire que ma réforme personnelle, dont je marque ici l'époque, qui m'attira leur jalousie [de ses soi-disans amis]: ils m'auroient pardonné peut-être de briller dans l'art d'écrire; mais ils ne purent me pardonner de donner par ma conduite un exemple qui sembloit les importuner. J'etois né pour l'amitié, mon humeur facile et douce la nourrissoit sans peine. Tant que je vécus ignoré du public je fus aimé de tous ceux qui me connurent, et je n'eus pas un seul ennemi. Mais sitot que j'eus un nom je n'eus plus d'amis.

The movement of the passage is very striking, for the last sentence appears to contradict the first. For Jean-Jacques Rousseau, citizen of Geneva, however, possession of a name entailed an obligation to exemplify the severe principles it expressed

Thus the trap had been sprung. The gaze of the world had been fixed on Rousseau, and he had to fulfil claims he had made in all innocence. Bravely, albeit slowly, he faced the task, and got rid of his fancy attire, his sword, his wig and his watch. Only one thing remained, his Venetian shirts, and fate helped him there: Thérèse's brother stole them. Rousseau has again altered the calendar, this time so as to bring together all the aspects of the personal reform. The theft was reported to the police, who took official note of it; it occurred on 25 December 1751 (Leigh app.77-app.79). In other words, the vestimentary reform, placed by Rousseau immediately after the publication of the *Discours*, took a full year to complete. Furthermore, the decision to resign as Francueil's cashier has been advanced to this period from 1752, for the same purpose.

The execution of the personal reform encountered obstacles, which delayed its full accomplishment. First of all, Rousseau's bad health continued to distract him. The reprise of this theme here cannot be challenged for veracity; Rousseau was ill much of the time. On the other hand, the very permanence of his condition makes its appearance in any given situation arbitrary. Having served to mark the depth of his depravity in Paris, and to cast the burden of responsibility for the first *Discours* onto Diderot, the illness now excuses the slowness of Rousseau's completion of the reform.

A second obstacle was what Rousseau termed 'occupations litteraires' (i.365), by which he meant the polemical battles in which he engaged after the first *Discours*. Both the literary occupations and the illness were well within Rousseau's own control, however, once he understood his situation clearly. Having despaired of regaining his good health, but also having outlived Morand's six-month deadline, Rousseau laid up a vast supply of catheters and returned to his copywork. Similarly, realizing that his pamphleteering 'm'occupoit beaucoup, avec beaucoup de perte de tems pour ma copie, peu de progrès pour la vérité et peu de profit pour ma bourse' (i.366), he wrote a last reply to Borde in April 1752 and quit.

The third obstacle was the most treacherous: Parisian society lionized Rousseau: (i.367):

Le sucçés de mes premiers Ecrits m'avoit mis à la mode. L'état que j'avois pris excitoit la curiosité: L'on vouloit connoitre cet homme bizarre qui ne recherchoit personne et ne se soucioit de rien que de vivre libre et heureux à sa maniére: c'en étoit assez pour qu'il ne le put point. Ma chambre ne desemplissoit pas de gens qui sous divers pretextes venoient s'emparer de mon tems. Les femmes employoient mille ruses pour m'avoir à diner. Plus je brusquois les gens, plus ils s'obstinoient. Je ne pouvois refuser tout le monde.

Mme de Graffigny of course entered his life at just this moment, under just those conditions. Perhaps Rousseau regarded *Les Saturnales* as a ruse to get him to dinner. In the next paragraph he describes his policy of refusing all gifts, with no exceptions (i.367):

Tout cela ne fit qu'attirer les donneurs qui vouloient avoir la gloire de vaincre ma resistance et me forcer de leur être obligé malgré moi. Tel qui ne m'auroit pas donné un écu si je l'avois demandé ne cessoit de m'importuner de ses offres, et pour se venger de les voir rejettées taxoit mes refus d'arrogance et d'ostentation.

If he is not referring to the comte de Clermont, it must have been to someone very much like him.

According to Rousseau, his new social prominence had two results. The first was to subject him to constant importunities, not only from would-be hostesses, but also from Thérèse and her mother, and from his friends. This in turn soured his mood. Having to think and work by the moment, he took to jotting his notes in a little book. In short 'Voila comment les désagrémens imprévus d'un état de mon choix me jettérent par diversion tout à fait dans la litterature, et voila comment je portai dans tous mes premiers ouvrages la bile et l'humeur qui m'en faisoient occuper' (i.368). In the next paragraph, he extends the principle to his social behaviour: 'Ma sote et maussade timidité que je ne pouvois vaincre ayant pour principe la crainte de manquer aux bienseances, je pris pour m'enhardir, le parti de les fouler aux pieds. Je me fis cynique et caustique par honte; j'affectai de mépriser la politesse que je ne savois pas pratiquer.' There is good evidence, however, in the *Confessions* as well as in mme de Graffigny's and mme d'Epinay's writings, to suggest that Rousseau was still quite sociable for most of this initial phase. The entire two-page development on his awkwardness must be regarded as an anticipatory apology for events that took place mainly in late 1752, 1753, and early 1754 – that is, after *Le Devin du village*, and after the passive attitude had been replaced by an active one.

If the first *Discours* is played down by Rousseau, *Le Devin du village* is given the place of honour in book viii. Writes Rousseau: '*Le Devin du village* acheva de me mettre à la mode, et bientot il n'y eut pas d'homme plus recherché que moi dans Paris. L'histoire de cette Piéce, qui fait époque, tient à celle des liaisons que j'avois pour lors. C'est un détail dans lequel je dois entrer pour l'intelligence de ce qui doit suivre' (i.369). There follows a long development on Rousseau's friendships at the time: Raynal, Grimm, Duclos, mme d'Epinay, d'Holbach, mme de Créqui, Saurin, the vicar of Marcoussis, Mussard; but whereas in the first part of book viii similar details distracted Rousseau's attentions from the *Discours* and interrupted the narrative flow, here he presents them as building toward the central point of the story, the conception of *Le Devin*, its production, and its consequences.

As with the *Discours*, Rousseau played a very passive role at the beginning. Inspiration came overnight; the applause of Mussard and mlle Du Vernois to whom he could not help showing the tunes, made him go on; Duclos then presented the work to the opera; and finally m. de Cury and the duc d'Aumont used their authority as royal spokesmen to have it put on at Fontainebleau. So far, it is a familiar story, but Rousseau has been leading to a crisis, which he now underscores: 'Me voici dans un de ces momens critiques de ma vie où il est difficile de ne faire que narrer, parce qu'il est presque impossible que la narration même ne porte empreinte de censure ou d'apologie' (i.377).

Rousseau relives the performance with a luxury of details, and then explains his decision to return to Paris rather than appear before the king. He is quite candid about the timidity and fear of appearing foolish that first frightened him, but does not for all that consider the principles he relied on to be invalidated. To have accepted the king's pension would have meant servitude; Rousseau preferred his freedom.

Rousseau dates his first quarrel with Diderot from this incident, and a number of other troubles as well. A full year is compressed into a few lines, as he recalls the persecutions that resulted from his *Lettre sur la musique française*, of November 1753. In the end, *Le Devin* 'fut le germe des secretes jalousies qui n'ont éclatté que longtemps après. Depuis son succés je ne remarquai plus ni dans Grimm ni dans Diderot ni dans presque aucun des gens de lettres de ma connoissance cette cordialité, cette franchise, ce plaisir de me voir que j'avois cru trouver en eux jusqu'alors' (i.386). There is reliable evidence to prove that Rousseau was wrong to suspect Diderot of jealousy in this episode, but it seems very likely that all his friends were shocked by his flight from Fontainebleau, and regarded him as somewhat deranged. It is certainly true that his *Lettre sur la musique française* was intemperate and heavy-handed, and that it brought real harassment, such as jostling by the crowd at the opera and eventually the denial of his right to entry, maybe even threats upon his life.

We must recall that Rousseau had pinned his initial hopes of success on his music. His earliest disappointment had been the refusal of the Academy to accept his new proposal for musical notation. His quarrel with Voltaire began with their collaboration on an opera in 1745, when Voltaire slighted Rousseau. Moreover, in later years Rousseau still placed his music highest among his accomplishments, and in *Rousseau juge de Jean-Jacques* he returned repeatedly to the theme in such remarks as 'Jean-Jacques était né pour la Musique' (*Œuvres*, i.872). In fact, his anxiety went back to his youthful years of wandering, his association with Venture de Villeneuve, and the concert for m. de Treitorens, the memory of which came back to him in the midst of his triumph at Fontainebleau.

To sum up the second phase of the reform, then, it began in 1752 as the first phase was ending and lasted until early 1754 in the aftermath of the *Querelle des Bouffons*. It was intensely focused on the *Devin du village*, the success of which meant far more to Rousseau than either of his *Discours*, and perhaps more than any of his other works. The gesture of refusing the king's audience and pension marked the change from a passive to an active stance; Rousseau assumed full responsibility for the act. Even with respect to public opinion and the attitude of his friends, he may well be right to make this the turning point, since the act was so bizarre and so visible. At this point, the intellectual progress has not been great; but the personal reform has passed its climax.

The final section of book viii describes the implementation of the reform, which took the form of a retreat, largely into the past; in this isolation, the intellectual reform would be carried out and related in book ix. At first, the incidents which make up the end of book viii seem disparate and disordered. The first one, the performance of *Narcisse*, took place in December 1752, not long after the performance of *Le Devin* at Fontainebleau, and well before the *Lettre sur la musique*. But if music was the unifying theme before, Rousseau's 'system' as he calls it, is the new one. After the première of *Narcisse* Rousseau again startled the literary world by openly claiming authorship of an anonymous flop, as he himself admitted; this gesture was a continuation of the active drive toward authenticity begun at Fontainebleau. Rousseau attached little importance to the play, but in publishing the text in early 1753 he added a preface, which, he says 'est un de mes bons écrits', and in which 'je commençai de mettre à découvert mes principes un peu plus que je n'avois fait jusqu'alors' (*Œuvres*, ii.388).

Next, he tells of reading the announcement of the new Dijon prize subject, which appeared in the *Mercure* in November 1753, and of his trip to Saint Germain to meditate on the *Discours sur l'origine de l'inégalité*. On his return, he resolved to stop looking to doctors for health, and he withdrew from the cabals and battles of the Parisian literary world. Diderot gave him a lot of advice on the *Discours sur l'origine de l'inégalité*, which in retrospect Rousseau deemed mischievously intended to darken and harden his tone, although that criticism would seem applicable primarily to the *Lettre sur la musique* which Rousseau wrote on his own. As we have just seen, the worst trials at the opera were taking place at exactly the same time as this resumption of Rousseau's intellectual life. In the midst of it, surely no one, least of all Rousseau himself, could have so neatly separated the strands of his evolving character and thought, as he does in the *Confessions*; but in retrospect, the bickering of the literary milieu, the harassment of the partisans of French music, and Diderot's over-solicitous encouragement all belonged to a receding stage, whereas the new *Discours* was the first and long-awaited glimmer of a glorious inner vision that would shine ever clearer for several years to come.

The renewal, of course, remained largely hidden. No one recognized the genius of the preface to *Narcisse*, only the eccentricity. The second *Discours*, composed during the winter of 1753-1754, did not appear in print until 1755. In the meanwhile, Rousseau completed his personal reform with a literal return to his past and to his origins. In June 1754 he made a trip to Geneva, where he formally regained the title of citizen that he had been using since 1750. On the way, he paid a visit to mme de Warens, whom he had never ceased to love and idealize.

Rousseau experienced the two-year period from early 1754 until 1756 as one of peace, optimism, and reintegration. He returned to Paris in October 1754 with a long list of writing projects begun or outlined: the *Institutions politiques*, a history of the Valais, a tragedy about Lucretia, and a translation of Tacitus. Mme d'Epinay offered him a retreat at the Hermitage, which Rousseau had admired and wished for, and which he accepted with tears of gratitude and affection. He repaid the favour in part by introducing mme d'Epinay to Tronchin, whom she wanted to consult. He sought a reconciliation with d'Holbach, on the occasion of mme d'Holbach's death. In the winter of 1755-1756, Palissot satirized him in the play *Les Originaux*, and Rousseau took the occasion to write magnanimously to king Stanislas on Palissot's behalf. These final signs of the reform's completion are narrated with the greatest economy. Much has been omitted, but the impression of a new stability and calm is clear. Even bad news and disappointments did not disturb Rousseau's equanimity, whether it be the failure of *Narcisse*, the poor reception of his *Discours* in Geneva, Voltaire's establishment in Geneva, or Palissot's satire.

This is all the more remarkable because in many respects the return to the past had been a failure. Mme de Warens had appeared in an appalling state of degradation. His old friend Gauffecourt had betrayed him, by making indecent advances to Thérèse. On his return to Paris, Rousseau imagined that he wanted to return to Geneva to live, but it is obvious that he had not been welcomed as he had hoped, and new pretexts easily deterred him. Then, unexpectedly, Venture de Ville-neuve came to see him; but he like Maman had lost his former charm, and Rousseau responded coldly. When he had gone, though, the whole series of memories of Rousseau's youth came back to him: 'toutes ces tendres réminiscences me firent verser des larmes sur ma jeunesse écoulée et sur ces transports désormais perdus pour moi' (i.399).

Rousseau's reform had had the strange result of cutting him off from time altogether. Having first broken with the present, he sought to return to his past, only to find it pathetically degraded. He retreated more and more into a fantasy world of idealized memories, and of course by the time he wrote the *Confessions* he knew how much he would suffer from the world's lack of understanding. The closing paragraphs of book viii are an appeal to the future, to a posterity that would not even begin until after Rousseau's death. Then, perhaps, he would be known 'tel qu'il fut réellement' (i.400).

IX

From life to literature

Such human realities are no doubt forever inexpressible in their
entirety; certainly Rousseau mistrusted the power of language to render
his thought fully and accurately. Yet the *Confessions* attain an un-
precedented degree of vividness because of the richness of the narrative
text. I have argued that, viewed from afar, the period between 1749
and 1756 seems well characterized as 'Rousseau's reform'; the illumination of Vincennes provides the dramatic turning point, which
reaches its conclusion with Rousseau's retreat to the Hermitage. A
closer inspection reveals many inconsistencies in that version; but I
have shown that the *Confessions* successfully work the apparently
disparate and incoherent events into a more complex but nonetheless
still rational pattern or plot. If a detailed chronology or a modern
psychology prevent our accepting some of Rousseau's notions of
causation, yet attention to the thematic and tonal qualities of the
incidents he associates makes clear that he has related the story with
equal care for orderly explanation and for truthful exposition of the
facts.

So much we may term conscious and deliberate; it is time now to
turn our attention to elements that seem to be unconscious and intuit-
ive, those aspects which strike us as illogical and eccentric, which
offend our sense of order. Such studies have been done before, and
each one no doubt owes as much to the idiosyncratic interests of the
critic as to the text itself. Such readings are, moreover, probably
limitless in number. I propose then neither to supplant earlier interpretations nor to exhaust the text of its meanings. Rather, this commentary grows out of my preoccupation with certain factual details,
supplements the insights I have garnered from previous readers, and
provides an exegesis of book viii compatible with my own convictions.

One of the most remarkable aspects of this chapter, to which notice
has already been drawn, is the lack of space given to the illumination
of Vincennes. Rousseau himself recognized it, indeed he emphasizes
it by digressing on the subject of his memory (*Œuvres*, i.351):

Quoique j'aye un souvenir vif de l'impression que j'en receus, les détails
m'en sont échappés depuis que je les ai déposés dans une de mes quatre

lettres à M. de Malesherbes. C'est une des singularités de ma mémoire qui méritent d'être dites. Quand elle me sert ce n'est qu'autant que je me suis reposé sur elle, sitot que j'en confie le dépot au papier elle m'abandonne, et dés qu'une fois j'ai écrit une chose je ne m'en souviens plus du tout. Cette singularité me suit jusques dans la musique. Avant de l'apprendre je savois par cœur des multitudes de chansons: sitot que j'ai su chanter des airs notés je n'en ai pu retentir aucun, et je doute que de ceux que j'ai le plus aimés j'en pusse aujourd'hui redire un seul tout entier.

Memory is a natural subject for an autobiographer, and especially for one in Rousseau's position, writing from memory without the support of his notes and papers, as he explains at length in book vii (i.277-279). It is nonetheless startling that he should substitute this digression for the description of his intense emotional and physical reaction to the question proposed by the Dijon academy, which he does in fact relate in the letter to Malesherbes (i.1135-1137). His intuition, however, should be respected, and we must consider memory and forgetfulness a theme perhaps more central to the reform, than the philosophical system born on the road to Vincennes.

As we have just seen, it is in fact the case that the reform ends in a resurgence of lost memories. The Pléiade editors underscore how much the second *Discours* owes to this factor: ' presque tout le *Discours* [. . .] est soulevé par un élan de nostalgie vers un état d'enfance' (i.1452). The illumination itself was a remembrance of a forgotten self, and the crucial problem for Rousseau was not how to develop in logical terms the implications of his paradox, but how to preserve the substance as well as the form of the memory and how to reawaken similar memories in others.

The pattern established in the first digression on memory holds true throughout book viii: Rousseau's memory fails in social contexts. The recollection, so long as it stayed locked inside him as unrecorded experience, stayed alive; once he transcribed it into written form, he lost it. Similarly, tunes learned through the direct imitation of musical sounds survived only so long as he did not learn a system of musical notation. On the eve of his audience with the king, Rousseau imagined the scene: he would be 'sous les yeux de toute la Cour', prisoner of the same unfamiliar etiquette and formality that had made him wonder during the performance 'si j'étois à ma place, si j'y étois mis convenablement? et après quelques minutes d'inquiétude, je me répondis, oui, avec une intrépidité qui venoit peut-être plus de l'impossibilité de m'en dédire que de la force de mes raisons' (i.377-378). Not only has the possibility now been given to him to withdraw, but also the conditions have grown more threatening: the king might speak to him, he would have to respond appropriately. 'Pour préparer d'avance une réponse heureuse, il auroit fallu prévoir juste ce qu'il pourroit me dire, et j'étois sûr après cela de ne pas retrouver en sa présence un mot de ce que j'aurois médité' (i.380). In short, Rousseau believed his instinctive response would be improper, a 'balourdise'; but his memory could not be trusted to work on the codes of language and social ceremony. The same accident befell him in fact when he went to Geneva, and had to appear before the commission to make his profession of faith: 'ayant étudié jour et nuit pendant trois semaines un petit discours que j'avois préparé, je me troublai lorsqu'il fallut le réciter au point de n'en pouvoir pas dire un seul mot, et je fis dans cette conférence le rolle du plus sot écolier' (i.393).

Indeed, the slightest rituals of civilization sufficed to erase Rousseau's memory. Explaining how he composed the first *Discours*, once again he treats it as a question of memory work (i.352):

Je méditois dans mon lit à yeux fermés, et je tournois et retournois mes périodes dans ma tête avec des peines incroyables; puis quand j'étois parvenu à en être content, je les déposois dans ma mémoire jusqu'à ce que je pusse les mettre sur le papier: mais le tems de me lever et de m'habiller me faisoit tout perdre, et quand je m'étois mis à mon papier, il ne me venoit presque plus rien de ce que j'avois composé. Je m'avisai de prendre pour Secretaire Made le Vasseur. [...] je lui dictois de mon lit mon travail de la nuit, et cette pratique, que j'ai longtems suivie m'a sauvé bien des oublis

Memory is, for Rousseau, one of the voices of nature, like conscience and tears. It belongs to, and preserves, the pure origins, of the self and of humanity. Quite predictably, it is associated with new beginnings, especially awakenings, where cliché supports the image: when Rousseau hears that he has won the prize, he says 'Cette nouvelle réveilla toutes les idées qui me l'avoient dicté' (i.356); the first inspiration for *Le Devin* came during the night, and 'Le matin en me promenant [always propitious to Rousseau's thinking] et en prenant les eaux je fis quelques maniéres de vers très à la hâte' (i.374). As a natural force, however, memory cannot be controlled; its eruption may disturb as well as console, as in the case of the reminiscences at the end of book viii.

The very last sentence of book viii relates the theme of memory to Rousseau's own image: 'Si ma mémoire devoit s'éteindre avec moi, plustot que de compromettre personne je souffrirois un opprobre injuste et passager sans murmure: mais puisqu'enfin mon nom doit vivre je dois tâcher de transmettre avec lui le souvenir de l'homme infortuné qui le porta, tel qu'il fut réellement, et non tel que d'injustes ennemis travaillent sans relâche à le peindre' (i.400). True memory is good, as Rousseau never stops reminding the reader of the *Confessions*, even though it portray the flaws of its subject. The *Confessions* express on every page the anguish of a consciousness fighting to preserve true memory against oblivion and distortion; and the illumination of Vincennes was, for Rousseau, less an intellectual perception than a pang of the heart over the things he had forgotten and perhaps lost forever.

The lowest point to which Jean-Jacques sank, in his own moral view, was the orgy with Klupfell's mistress, of which he says: 'Les propos et le vin nous égayèrent au point que nous nous oubliames' (ii.354-355). Unfortunately for humanity, the enjoyment of self-abandonment and the enthusiasm of virtue are not always easy to distinguish. Book viii is the story of a man in a continuous state of exaltation, and in some ways a study of the forms it may assume. The book begins with Rousseau close to madness because of Diderot's imprisonment; when Diderot received permission to see his friends, Rousseau rushed to him and despair turned to equally delirious joy: 'En entrant je ne vis que lui, je ne fis qu'en saut, un cri, je collai mon visage sur le sien, je le serrai étroitement sans lui parler autrement que par mes pleurs et par mes sanglots; j'étouffois de tendresse et je joye' (i.350). His zeal to console his friend was such that he collapsed along the road to Vincennes, and of course he happened on the announcement of the prize competition because he had taken the *Mercure* to slow himself down. In the letter to Malesherbes, Rousseau recounts the many signs of inspiration he experienced immediately upon reading the question; in the *Confessions* he emphasizes that 'arrivant à Vincennes j'étois dans une agitation qui tenoit du délire' (i.351). Moreover, the condition persisted (i.351):

Mes sentiments se montérent avec la plus inconcevable rapidité au ton de mes idées. Toutes mes petites passions furent étouffées par l'enthousiasme de la vérité, de la liberté, de la vertu, et ce qu'il y a de plus étonnant est que cette effervescence se soutint dans mon cœur durant plus de quatre ou cinq ans à un aussi haut dégré peut être qu'elle ait jamais été dans le cœur d'aucun autre homme.

Not surprisingly, Rousseau's state of effervescence was ultimately good; but some of its analogues, especially in other men, were not. Sexuality permeates the *Confessions*, and is a common source of wrongful agitation. Rousseau's orgy is a case in point, contrasted specifically with the tranquil pleasures he shared with Thérèse. We must add to the list also the curious tale of Grimm's near-fatal passion for mademoiselle Fel, and Gauffecourt's disloyal attempts at seducing Thérèse on the journey to Geneva. As Rousseau had learned through painful experience by the time he wrote the *Confessions*, if not as he lived these moments, sexual drives had to be sublimated to serve virtue: witness Julie and Saint-Preux. Mme de Chenonceaux aroused Rousseau, in part by stimulating his memory: 'Ses cheveux d'un blond cendré et d'une beauté peu commune, me rappelloient ceux de ma pauvre Maman dans son bel âge, et m'agitoient vivement le cœur' (i.359), but he did nothing, though he does not know whether to call his behaviour 'sage' or 'fou'.

Eroticism played a great part in Rousseau's triumph on the first night of *Le Devin* at Fontainebleau: 'Je suis pourtant sûr qu'en ce moment la volupté du sexe y entroit beaucoup plus que la vanité d'auteur, et surement s'il n'y eut eu là que des hommes, je n'aurois pas été dévoré, comme je l'étois sans cesse du desir de recueillir de mes levres les delicieuses larmes que je faisois couler' (i.379). In this scene, the entire audience is swept away by what Rousseau terms 'fermentation' and 'ivresse'. To schematize, Rousseau depicts himself in three sexual roles: seducer, seduced, and enjoyer. To each, he contrasts a false version: Gauffecourt's calculating efforts to arouse Thérèse with pornography; Grimm's feigned illness; his own participation in the orgy out of shame. The erotic delirium may be an active principle of moral improvement, if it is spontaneous and sincere, and if it is contained by the will within the limits of morality.

By the same token, immunity from enthusiasm is morally bad, for it signifies resistance to the contagion of virtue. Rousseau agonizes over his own apparent failures, most notably over the abandonment of his children; a long passage on his acute *sensibilité* concludes (i.357):

Cet attendrissement, cette vive et douce émotion que je sens à l'aspect de tout ce qui est vertueux, généreux, aimable; tout cela peut-il jamais s'accorder dans la même âme avec la dépravation qui fait fouler aux pieds sans scrupule le plus doux des devoirs? Non, je le sens et le dis hautement; cela n'est pas possible. Jamais un seul instant de sa vie J. J. n'a pu être un homme sans sentiment, sans entrailles, un pere dénaturé.

In a sense, the intensity of his feelings on other matters guarantees the fundamental goodness of his feelings here.

All around, however, are examples of coldness. Grimm, most consistently, from their first meeting never gave evidence of warmth and spontaneity. Diderot, in response to Rousseau's passionate greeting in Vincennes, thought of how he could use it to his advantage – or so Rousseau interprets his remark in retrospect. After the success of *Le Devin*, Rousseau found 'ni dans Grimm ni dans Diderot ni dans presque aucun des gens de lettres de ma connoissance cette cordialité, cette franchise, ce plaisir de me voir que j'avois cru trouver en eux jusqu'alors' (i.386). By way of comparison, one should take note of Rousseau's affection for m. Mussard, who is described as virtually insane: 'Toujours occupé de cet objet et de ses singuliéres découvertes, il s'échauffa si bien sur ces idées qu'elles se seroient enfin tournées dans sa tête en systéme, c'est à dire, en folie' (i.373). The warmth and sincerity of the conviction, mad though it was, sufficed to draw Rousseau close to him.

Rousseau, his mind in turmoil, gradually cut himself off from most of his former friends by 1756, and usually cited their lack of feelings as a pretext. As with the abandonment of his children, however, it was always his own failure to respond that troubled him most, and just such a failure seems to have provoked the final crisis. First came his reunion with mme de Warens, about whom he writes (i.391-392):

Il falloit tout quitter pour la suivre, m'attacher à elle jusqu'à sa derniére heure, et partager son sort quel qu'il fut. Je n'en fis rien. Distrait par un autre attachement, je sentis relâcher le mien pour elle, faute d'espoir de pouvoir le lui rendre utile. Je gémis sur elle et ne la suivis pas. De tous les remords que j'ai sentis en ma vie voila le plus vif et le plus permanent. Je méritai par là les châtiments terribles qui depuis lors n'ont cessé de m'accabler; puissent-elles avoir expié mon ingratitude. Elle fut dans ma conduite, mais elle a trop déchiré mon cœur pour que jamais ce cœur ait été celui d'un ingrat.

As with the many other occasions in his life when the superlatively intense regrets were provoked, it is less the deed itself, than the apparent lack of feeling that Rousseau seeks to excuse. Of course this has the convenient corollary that the strength of his feelings after the event can compensate for his apathy at the time. This is not to impugn his sincerity nor to belittle the system of values he is implicitly advocating. He has located the problem of morality where it is no doubt best confronted: in the failure of the heart to ratify the dictates of the moral law. In this, as perhaps in most cases, the application of moral law stems originally from a commitment of the heart; the ingratitude Rousseau regrets was specifically the failure of his feelings to stay true to themselves.

The reappearance of Venture de Villeneuve had a similar effect on Rousseau; if he had no debts of gratitude toward his former idol, he was nonetheless troubled by his lack of response. 'Qu'il me parut changé! Au lieu de ses anciennes graces je ne lui trouvai plus qu'un air crapuleux, qui m'empêcha de m'épanouir avec lui. Ou mes yeux n'étoient plus les mêmes, ou tout son prémier éclat tenoit à celui de la jeunesse qu'il n'avoit plus. Je le vis presque avec indifférence, et nous nous séparames assez froidement' (i.398). But if the real Venture de Villeneuve left Rousseau unmoved, he served to revive the image of the days when they were friends, and in solitude Rousseau felt that flood of emotion he had missed at the time. As he recalls his past, it is a list of erotic ecstasies that he relates: his days with mme de Warens, who is compared to Venture de Villeneuve in terms of degradation; the day spent at Toune with mlle de Graffenried and mlle Galley, the 'jouissance', the 'regrets si vifs', the 'ravissans délires'; and in the end Rousseau weeps 'sur ma jeunesse écoulée et sur ces transports désormais perdus pour moi' (i.398-399). What has been lost, apparently, is a capacity to feel.

Feelings and memory are then bound together in book viii. Ready access to both is a sign of goodness, for both come from nature and are repressed or replaced in society by artificial expressions. What Rousseau saw on the road to Vincennes was his lost natural self, and the possibility of its recovery. When he writes, 'A l'instant de cette lecture je vis un autre univers et je devins un autre homme' (i.351), he is describing a genuine split within himself. It was painful enough to renounce the socialized personality that had been imposed on him by his years of struggling to succeed in Paris; painful enough to confront the jeers of his enemies and jests of his friends; painful enough to break through again to the submerged feelings and memories that he suddenly realized still lived inside him. What he had perhaps not foreseen was that all the different Rousseaus, authentic and denatured, true and false, would go on living together, and not merely within his mind and soul, but with an independent life of their own over which he had no control.

The *Confessions* do not mention the exchange of letters with Voltaire in 1750, but that incident posed the issue of Rousseau's identity to him as bluntly as possible. Pierre Rousseau was a kind of substitute for Jean-Jacques, a namesake at loose in the world for whose acts Jean-Jacques might be called to account. Moreover, as he wrote to Voltaire, Jean-Jacques compounded the problem by invoking still another image of himself, the one which he supposed Voltaire to have held; and then another, the one he held of himself and described as citizen of Geneva.

Jean Starobinski has written some brilliant pages on Rousseau's use of his names as a method of regeneration. As he called himself mr. Dudding or Vaussore de Villeneuve, he expected the title to endow him with its mystical qualities. Having enfolded himself in the role, he would thereby both force himself and enable himself to live up to it. So too with the title of citizen of Geneva; having taken it, somewhat improperly, Rousseau then undertook to deserve it. In the letter to Voltaire, he returns repeatedly to the theme of his qualities and title, in both a literal and metaphoric sense – that is to say, his identity under civil law, and his moral right to appear before Voltaire.

The reformative powers of a self-imposed title differ, however, from the anxieties produced by the mysterious rumours of usurped selves circulating elsewhere. The focal point of this book is, as already noted, the story of *Le Devin du village*. At the very heart of that story, Rousseau relates one of the most dramatic instances of his anxiety before his false double: On the very day of the triumphant first performance, in a café at Fontainebleau, Rousseau overheard an officer who claimed to have been at the rehearsal of *Le Devin* and to know the author. This impostor 'dépeignit l'Auteur, rapporta ce qu'il avoit fait, ce qu'il avoit dit' (i.376). The most remarkable aspect, as Rousseau rightly remarks, was his own reaction: instead of confronting the impostor, Rousseau felt guilty and slunk out of the café in terror lest he be recognized, claiming as his motive his sympathy for the liar: 'je suis sûr que si quelqu'un m'eut reconnu et nommé avant ma sortie, on m'auroit vu la honte et l'embarras d'un coupable, par le seul sentiment de la peine que ce pauvre homme auroit à souffrir si son mensonge étoit reconnu' (i.377).

Rousseau's excessive identification with this impostor betrays his own fears of being an impostor. The phantom author of *Le Devin* must have been a figure Jean-Jacques had imagined long before he heard the officer mention him. There *were* borrowings in the opera, as he confesses in the *Dialogues*: Collé's words to a song, Cahusac's words to an ariette, and an air supplied treacherously by d'Holbach; moreover, Francueil and Jelyotte had written a new recitatif. Indeed, the sudden inspirational composition of *Le Devin* left him vulnerable to the possibility that involuntary memories had influenced his work. The parallel to an earlier concert at which he had tried to pass for a composer did not escape him; in the midst of the performance, he tells us, 'J'eus un moment de retour sur moi-même en me rappellant le concert de M. de Treitorens' (i.379).

Rousseau escaped from the café at Fontainebleau by annihilating himself, as the Pléiade editors put it. It is only one of his selves that has been annihilated, though; the sheepish schoolboy survived, as did the phantom author, and perhaps the plagiarist. It was the successful author-composer who was destroyed, because even Rousseau was unsure of that self's existence. The officer in the café, bearing all the symbols of paternal authority – advanced age, respectable bearing, cross of Saint-Louis, self-assurance – became an objectification of Rousseau's self-doubts.

Music had long been Rousseau's main hope, and remained an obsession throughout his life. It is fitting, then, that the recall of the concert of m. de Treitorens should be followed by the return of a key figure from that era: Venture de Villeneuve. He had been the model for Rousseau's pseudonym, Vaussore de Villeneuve, and for his behaviour in presenting himself as a composer. He was a literal alter ego for Jean-Jacques, whose crapulous condition added to, but did not really cause Rousseau's dismay at the sight of him. He was the spectre of a past Rousseau would have preferred to forget, a youth not pure, not authentic, but already contaminated by the pretences and ambitions he was giving up.

And there was worse still. Rousseau had not of course *been* Venture de Villeneuve, but had been his companion. When Venture came to see him, 'Un autre homme était avec lui' (i.398), says Rousseau without comment; but it is a curious echo of the dramatic 'Je devins un autre homme' at the beginning of book viii; and the role this other man is playing makes further commentary superfluous on Rousseau's part. In becoming 'other' in the 1750s, Rousseau had meant to go back, to slough off false appearances and recover a pristine innocence from the past. Counterfeits plagued him, first as false images of what he had become, then as false images of what he had been. The only reliable past, the only reliable feelings and memories, the only reliable self had to be found within.

The process of change, rebirth, and regeneration, functions in ways distressingly similar to less desirable passions. Ugly lust, gross sensual appetites, illness and madness can produce delirious enthusiasms like those of truth and virtue. An immense effort of the will is required to be sure that one follows the voice of nature, not the seductive rationalizations of a denatured self. The journey within is as arduous as any, but it is the only route to salvation. The corruptions of society are such that nothing in the present or the past can be relied on, except for what remains within, the feelings and the nostalgia of the original innocent state. Thus it is that at the end of the reform, Rousseau must make his appeal outside of time altogether. He himself retreated into an imaginary or idealized past; but he had left in his wake many other selves that continued to haunt him. The full horror of his predicament did not become clear to him until later, after the 'infernal affair' and the break with Diderot, after his exile and the slanders of Voltaire. Then he would feel the need to oppose to this gallery of false and fragmented selves the one true portrait that would overwhelm them, and preserve his memory as it truly was, forever.

The Graffigny papers contain several versions of *Les Saturnales*. The fragment by Rousseau is in GP, lxxxi.61-64. In GP, xciii.231-270, there is a version which answers the description of the text by Destouches; it is briefer and has fewer characters than the final version. Moreover, the plot is focused heavily on Caton's sister Servilie, an ageing coquette who foolishly believes that César loves her, and who is ridiculed by everyone at the end when César wins the hand of Cornélie. Dromon, the articulate slave, plays little role; Cornélie, the virtuous girl, hardly appears on stage; even Caton, the mainspring of the comedy in mme de Graffigny's mind, has almost nothing to say or do. Whether the quality of the writing is as far below the final product as mme de Graffigny claims is debatable; but if hers is no masterpiece either, at least it is better suited to its intended audience of children, and to its purpose of edification.

The Bibliothèque nationale possesses a partial draft of *Les Saturnales* in Bret's hand (N. a. fr.9209, ff.311-316). It represents an early version; César, for example, appears in only two scenes (ii.ii-iii), and Cornélie does not appear at all. Bret's writing is very hasty, with many corrections; moreover, he used the empty margins as fresh pages toward the end, so that the sequence is very hard to follow. Act I is almost entirely devoted to a scene between Caton and Dromon; this scene (i.iv) was still far too long and monotonous in Bret's final draft, so mme de Graffigny added a scene with Davus (GP, lxxxi.14, and see the note). Act II in this manuscript is constructed very much as it appears in Bret's final draft, but act III is barely begun (see the note to GP, xc.53-58).

In GP, xci.1-127, there is a complete text in a fair copy, obviously the work of a professional copyist. It is very close to the text I have transcribed here, but is not identical to it. I believe that it represents a revision undertaken in 1755; on 29 June of that year, mme de Graffigny wrote to Devaux, 'Les puissances se disputent mes petites pieces et enfin je suis apres a les faire copier. Les collations de ses miseres me mangent un tems qui me desole. J'en pers beaucoup aussi a corriger les Saturnales qui me font mal au cœur par leurs longueurs et langueur' (GP, lxii.122). By usual editing standards, this would obviously be the preferred text. I have chosen an earlier one for several reasons: it represents mme de Graffigny's conception of the play in 1752, when she was working with Rousseau, rather than her afterthoughts of three years later; the manuscript is a working copy, showing her corrections of Bret's text, so that it is possible to determine with some accuracy how much of the play is really mme de Graffigny's; the 1752 play was the one which was sent to Vienna and put on. The Oester-reichische Nationalbibliothek in Vienna owns a manuscript of *Les Saturnales* (ser. nov. 2694, no.220), with the indication on the title-page that it was performed in 1752 by a cast of archdukes and archduchesses; there are only minor variants from mme de Graffigny's manuscript.

The text which follows, then, is taken from GP, lxxxi.1-60 and GP, xc.53-58. The first and longer part consists of pages divided into two columns, much like Rousseau's fragment. Bret's text is written, in a clear and easily legible copyist's hand, on the left side only. Mme de Graffigny then made corrections by crossing out parts, writing small changes between the lines, and adding long passages in the right hand columns. The last three scenes, bound in the other volume, are entirely in mme de Graffigny's hand. She, too, wrote only in the left hand column, leaving room for revisions on the right; but only a small number were actually made on this manuscript.

I have used the following signs: brackets [ ] indicate passages crossed out by mme de Graffigny; where nothing was substituted, I have put [x] to indicate less than a line cut, and [xxx 3 lines] to indicate three lines cut. Passages added by mme de Graffigny are enclosed within superior italic *, and are also enclosed within the brackets if they are to replace passages crossed out. The volume and page numbers of the manuscript are enclosed within brackets.

Les Saturnales

Comédie en trois actes
par Mme de Graffigny

ACTEURS

CATON

CÉSAR

SERVILIE, sœur de Caton

CORNÉLIE, fille de Cinna

CINNA, père de Cornélie

BACCHIS, suivante de Servilie

SOSTRATA, nourrice de Cornélie

DROMON, esclave de Caton

CRATINUS, affranchi de César

Troupe d'enfants

Troupe d'esclaves

LES SATURNALES

Comedie en trois actes

ACTE Ier

Une troupe d'enfants traverse le theatre en criant: Saturnales Saturnales.

Scene 2^e

Les Esclaves arrivent en foule en repetant le même cri. Ils forment des danses violentes qui expriment la joie effrenée du peuple.

Scene 3^e

Caton, Dromon, les Esclaves

CATON

Que font ici ces miserables? quel bruit! quelle joie effrenée! [x] Sortés [^ad'ici vils esclaves, et que je ne sois jamais le temoin de l'abus que vous faites de la bonté des dieux.^a]
Les Esclaves s'enfuient avec tant de précipitation qu'ils tombent les uns sur les autres.

Scene 4^e

Caton, Dromon

DROMON

Ah ah ah ah les sots! [^ails^a] fuient [x], comme si la fête des Saturnales que les enfans viennent d'annoncer, ne les dispensoit pas de toute obeissance. Il n'y a que la morgue du redoutable Caton qui puisse en imposer dans un jour qui rétablit l'égalité parmi les hommes. [xxx 14 lines]

[81.3]   CATON
Temeraire!

                                         DROMON

Doucement, s'il vous plait. Les mots injurieux, et surtout les gestes vous sont interdits [x]. Nous sommes camarades, mon cher Patron, afin que vous le sachiés.

                            [*CATON

Ô Saturne peux-tu etre honnoré par une vile populasse qui ose s'egaler aux premiers des romains?*]

                                         DROMON

Oui, cela est facheux, [*j'en conviens*]. Comment donc perdre pour sept jours le droit inestimable de battre, d'injurier, de faire mourir même, si la fantaisie en prend, des [*infortunés*] soumis par la force des armes, et qui n'ont d'autre crime que celui d'étre malheureux, oh! cela est insoutenable, et je vous plains bien fort.

                                         CATON
Selerat! Tu oses me railler?

                                         DROMON

Si vous continués, je vais crier aux [*Saturnales et vous verez que j'ai droit de me divertir*].

                                         CATON

Eh! qui t'en empeche, miserable? vas, [81.4] rejoins tes compagnons, et livre-toi à la licence que la fête autorise.

                                         DROMON

Non pas, non pas, [*mon gout*] est [x] plus noble que celui de mes camarades. De tous les plaisirs [*dont cette fete me permet l'usage, je donne la preference a celui de vous instruire de vos devoirs. Peut-on rien de plus honnete?

CATON

M'instruire de mes devoirs, impudent!

DROMON

Oui. Je me sens cette année une tendresse pour vous que je n'avois pas les autres. Je veux vous faire connoitre les vertus que vous ignorez et surtout l'humanité que vous ne connoissez point du tout. En un mot je veux vous rendre homme de bien.ᵃ]

CATON

Donner des conseils à Caton, quelle audace!

DROMON

Croire n'en avoir pas besoin, quel orgueil!

CATON

Dromon! la fête ne dure que sept jours, tu devrois t'en souvenir.

DROMON

Caton, je suis votre égal, vous ne devés pas l'oublier. [x] Profités mieux que vous ne faites de l'institution des Saturnales.

[81.5]   CATON

Ah fort bien! le sage Dromon va conseiller à Caton de se méler aux danses effrenées de ses semblables.

DROMON

Vous n'en seriés que mieux, cela dérouilleroit un peu votre humeur farouche. Mais ce n'est pas de quoi il [ᵃs'agit. Il est question de prendre l'esprit de cette fete et de profiter des leçons qu'elle vous donne.

CATON

Cette fete regarde-t-elle un citoien tel que moi?

DROMON

Sans doute. J'en sais la dessus plus que vous. L'orgueil vous aveugle, et le malheur m'éclaire. Vous pensés que les Saturnales ne furent établies que pour *divertir* les misérables, que vous nommés [*vile populasse.

CATON

Et pour quoi donc?

DROMON

Pour vous faire souvenir a vous autres grands*] que du tems de Saturne les conditions étoient égales, [*et pour vous porter a etre plus humain, et je gage que parmis les Gaulois ou cette fete n'est point etablie les grands et les bourus comme vous restent incorrigibles.

[81.6]   CATON

Cela pouroit etre bon parmis des barbares tels que les Gaulois mais*] le renversement de l'ordre ne peut jamais rien produire [*que de facheux parmis les Romains*].

DROMON

Ô par Saturne! le renversement n'est pas du coté ou vous le voiés. Vous étes blessé de voir des esclaves devenir vos égaux; cependant rien n'est si naturel que de permettre à des malheureux opprimés de reprendre leurs droits et d'étre hommes pendant quelques jours. Mais d'obliger des maitres riches et par conséquent hauts impérieux et inhumains à redevenir hommes, à rentrer sous les loix de la nature, voilà ce terrible renversement que vous ne pouvés souffrir, et qui cependant peut vous étre plus utile qu'à personne.

CATON

[*A moi?*]

DROMON

[*Oui a vous meme. Je conois peu de Romains qui ait plus besoin que vous d'entendre les verités que vos esclaves*] [81.7] sont en droit de vous dire. Mes camarades sont des laches qui vous [*haissent*] autant qu'ils vous craignent. Moi j'ai du courage et je vous aime; [ᵃécoutez moi premierement.

Scene 5ᵉ

Caton, Dromon, Davus

DAVUS

Tu as menti, Dromon. J'aime le patron autant que toi et s'il ne faut que lui dire ses verités pour te le prouver tu va voir. Vous etes un brutal, un avare, un yvrogneᵃ].

CATON

Esclave temeraire, [ᵃje te ferai metre en piece.

DROMON

Tu es une bete, Davus, ne sais-tu pas qu'il ne faut jamais montrer la verité toute nuë? Et vous mon patron qui vous emportez au premier mot, voici votre leçon. Quelqu'un disoit a Jupiter, 'Tu prends ta foudre, donc tu as tort.'

CATON

Quoi, je soufrirois . . . Ah mille coups me vangeront.

DROMON

Quelque sage n'a-t-il pas dit aussi, 'Frape mais eccoute.'ᵃ]

CATON

Miserable es-tu digne de repeter de pareilles sentences?

DROMON

Apparemment, puisque je les applique à propos. Voilà encore une erreur des [x] orgueilleux. [ᵃIls croientᵃ] que la condition décide du bon sens, et qu'il n'est pas permis à un malheureux d'avoir [ᵃde la raison.

DAVUS

Tu dis bien, Dromon. Je t'aprouve mais laisse-moi de la place pour parler. Eh, tiens tiens, voila tout fini, le patron s'en va*].

[81.8]   DROMON

Ou allés-vous, *Caton*?

CATON

Tu es bien hardi de me le demander.

DROMON

Ce n'est pas pour le savoir. Je sais que vous voulés fuir la verité, mais il faut l'entendre. Et de la part de tous les dieux j'ordonne au pieux Caton de m'ecouter.

CATON

Le traitre abuse de mon respect pour [*la religion*]!

DROMON

Ah! Je savois bien que vous m'ecouteriés.

CATON

Eh bien! Parlés. Qu'as-tu à réprocher à Caton? Ne montre-t'il pas en toute occasion les sentimens d'un Romain?

DROMON

C'est à dire d'un homme, car malgré la folie de vos pareils, qui prétendent pour ainsi dire faire d'un Romain un ètre particulier, je vois tous les jours, à commencer par vous, qu'un Romain est un homme assujetti aux vices et aux deffauts de l'humanité, ainsi que le pauvre Dromon.

*DAVUS

Qu'il dit bien! Mais je ne l'entens pas.*

CATON

Le témoignage de la République suffit à mes vertus.

DROMON

La république entend vos harangues, et moi je vous vois. Par exemple, apparemment [ᵃque vous ne comptez pasᵃ] la modestie au nombre [ᵃde vosᵃ] vertus.

[81.9]   CATON

La modestie soutient les vertus obscures, les miennes sont connues. On m'accuseroit d'hypocrisie, si je parlois de moi comme un homme ordinaire doit parler de lui.

ᵃDAVUS

Dromon, coment cela se fait-il? Je ne suis pas sourd, et je n'entens pas mieux le patron que toi.

[DROMON

Tais-toi. (a Caton) Fort bien, mon maitre, fort bien. Instruisez-moi aᵃ] mon tour, et nommés-moi ces autres vertus qui dispensent de la modestie. Je suis curieux de les connoitre.

CATON

Je ne prétends pas pour cela en manquer. On voit assés par ma haine pour le luxe, et par la simplicité de mes vetements . . .

ᵃDAVUS

Pour le coup tu as tort. Vois comme il est vetu. Il fait compation.

[DROMON

Retairas tu. Vous n'en etes pas quite.ᵃ] La simplicité [ᵃdont vous vous vantez est unᵃ] mot trop honnète pour caracteriser votre malpropreté. Le grand Caton, il est vrai, ne se pare point, la pourpre de Tyr n'est pas plus precieuse à ses yeux que l'etoffe la plus grossiere, mais il étale ses haillons et sa malpropreté avec plus d'orgueil, je dirois presque de coquetterie, que nos jeunes Romains n'etalent leur parure. L'affectation est égale, il n'y a que l'objet qui differe.

[ᵃDAVUS

Je ne me serois jamais douté de cela.

123

CATON

Auroit-on pu croire que l'on reprocha a Caton de manquer de modestie dans ses vetemens.

DROMON

Oui et je vous soutiens que c'est dans l'indifference pour*] le luxe que consiste la modestie extérieure. Le sage ne se distingue ni par les haillons ni par la pourpre. Il se conforme à son etat et à sa condition.

CATON

Je suis curieux de savoir [*coment le raisonneur Dromon*] [81.10] pouroit aussi donner une tournure satirique à ma frugalité.

*DAVUS

A moi, a moi celui ci. Je le tiens. C'est avarice pure, ladrerie meme. Il n'y a qu'a voir la fraicheur de votre cuisine et la maigreur de vos esclaves.

[DROMON

Il a raison, mais il ne sait pas tout. Il ne sait pas que vous ne haissez la bonne*] chere que chez vous; [*et que*] le vin de Salerne, qui n'entra jamais dans vos selliers, vous renvoie souvent de chez vos amis [*tres*] bien conditionné.

*CATON

C'est la gourmandise qui parle par ta bouche.

[DROMON

Gourmandise si vous voulez, mais sans le secour du gourmand Dromon on trouveroit souvent le frugal Caton couché*] dans la rue au grand scandale de la philosophie et de la République.

[*CATON

Oh je n'y saurois plus tenir. Vils esclaves, il vous appartient bien de juger de l'ame de Caton, est-ce a vous a connoitre son courage a soutenir les droits de sa patrie et sa fermeté a deffendre la liberté romaine?*] [xxx 28 lines]

[81.11]   [*ᵃ*DROMON

Tenez, dussiez-vous me faire servir de nouriture aux lemproyes,
j'entre en fureur quand j'entens venter l'amour de la liberté a des*ᵃ*]
hommes qui tiennent dans l'esclavage autant de malheureux qu'ils
peuvent en soumettre par la violence.

*ᵃ*DAVUS

Et qui les maltraitent comme des betes.

[DROMON

Qui les condamnent aux emploix les plus vils et aux chatimens les*ᵃ*]
plus horribles pour les fautes les plus legeres. Voilà ces Romains
qui croient que les Dieux [81.12] etablirent la liberté pour eux seuls, et
leur donnerent le droit de subjuguer l'univers.

CATON

Dromon, Dromon, tu ne sais pas ce que tu te prépares.

DROMON

[*ᵃ*Et voila celui qui se croit le plus grand de tous et qui n'a de raison
pour se deffendre que des menaces.

CATON

Ah, s'en est trop. Sortez d'ici, canailles, ou vous eprouverez si l'on
m'insulte impunement.

DAVUS

Dromon, restes si tu peux pour moi. La peur m'en porte.

Scene 6ᵉ

Caton, Dromon

CATON

Tu ne sors point.

125

DROMON

Vous le voiez.

CATON

Quelle hardiesse! Va, cours a ton devoir et songe a contenir mes esclaves, et surtout que les portes de ma maison soient exactement fermées.ª] [xxx 42 lines]
[81.13] [xxx completely]
[81.14] Je m'en prendrai à toi, s'il entre chez moi des esclaves etrangers.

DROMON

Tout autant qu'il en viendra ils seront bien reçus. Je respecte les ordres des Dieux avant ceux de Caton. Allons, gay! Saturnales, Saturnales!

(*Il sort en sautant et en dansant*)

Scene 5ᵉ1

Caton, Servilie, Bacchis

SERVILIE

Ah! vous voilà, mon frere, j'en suis surprise.

CATON

Il est vrai que rien n'est si surprenant que de trouver un homme dans sa maison; quelle tête!

SERVILIE

ªAh queª vous voilà bien, [ªprenant toujoursª] de travers ªtoutª ce qu'on vous dit. N'aviés-vous pas parlé d'aller à la campagne pendant cette fête? Ne vouliés-vous pas vous epargner la douleur de voir les autres se divertir?

---

1 act I, scene v, should be I.vii. Mme de Graffigny added the character Davus to relieve the monotonous length of the scene between Caton and Dromon; his entrance and exit added two scenes, but the numbers were not corrected for later scenes in act I.

CATON

Si la sotise des hommes m'eloigne d'eux, leur intéret m'en raproche. On m'a donné avis de quelques mouvements séditieux qui pouroient s'augmenter à la faveur des Saturnales. C'est à Caton à veiller sur les entreprises de Cesar. Ce jeune ambitieux . . .

SERVILIE

est charmant, mon frere; il est le plus aimable de tous les Romains. Vous devriés finir vos [81.15] invectives contre lui, cela ne vous fait pas honneur.

CATON

Servilie! Ma mere vous donna la naissance; mais alors elle n'etoit point encore alliée à la famille des Catons, et vous me faites bien voir que leur sang ne coule pas dans vos veines.

SERVILIE

Pourquoi cela?

CATON

C'est que vous hairiés comme moi l'ennemi de la République.

SERVILIE

Moi que je haisse Cesar! [ᵃVoila une belle idée! Mais pourquoi seroit-il l'ennemi de laᵃ] République! Allés, [x] mon frere, vous ne vous y connoissés pas, il fait l'ornement des Romains, il en fera la gloire.

CATON

Si vos paroles avoient du poids, si elles n'étoient celles d'une insensée, je vous traiterois tout à l'heure ainsi que Brutus a traité son fils.

SERVILIE

Bon! Quelle folie! Vous me tueriés? Mais, mon frere, en supposant que je sois folle, vous seriés bien plus fou que moi, et vous n'y gagne-riés rien, car aprés ma mort je louerois encore Cesar.

CATON

Je vous laisse plus d'un Marius dans le jeune Cesar, disoit le criminel Sylla. Il prévoioit que ce temeraire joindroit l'art de séduire à l'ambition de commander. Mais, ma soeur, *est-ce a vous a le deffendre*, à votre age n'est-il pas tems d'ètre raisonnable?

[81.16]   SERVILIE

A mon age! à mon age! Entendés-vous, Bacchis? Il me trouve décrépite assurément. Ah! que [*la mechante humeur*] est un mauvais juge!

CATON

Caton ne juge jamais que sur la verité. Si vous n'ètes pas décrépite, au moins ètes-vous dans l'age de la raison.

SERVILIE

Je suis dans celui des plaisirs, mon frere, et si vous voulés me suivre pendant ces fêtes, vous apprendrés si je suis d'un age à m'ennuier. J'ai mille projets de divertissement les plus agreables, les plus riants, les plus gais du monde. Voulés-vous en ètre?

CATON

Quelle proposition! Mais [x] dans ces projets de plaisirs [*songez a n'y point faire*] entrer celui de recevoir des presents, suivant l'usage ridicule de cette fête.

BACCHIS

Le Patron a raison, madame, cet usage tire à consequence. On ne reçoit point sans ètre obligé de rendre, et cela est [*triste*].

SERVILIE

Avarice, mon frere, avarice.

CATON

Et surtout je vous recommande Cornelie. C'est un dépot sacré que m'a laissé son pere jusqu'a son retour. Il a choisi la maison de Caton comme la plus décente de Rome [*pour y mettre sa fille en sureté pendant son absence*a*]. [81.17] Il revient ce soir. Aiés soin que d'ici-là les esclaves n'abusent *a*pas*a* de leur liberté pour se familiariser avec elle.

SERVILIE

Ah! Vous n'avés rien à craindre. L'orgueil de cette petite personne sera un assés bon frein pour la deffendre. A son age elle [*a*fait la reservée, elle donne dans le sublime de la raison. Elle est bien grave, bien ridicule. Oh, cela doit vous*a*] la rendre bien prétieuse.

CATON

Plût aux Dieux que vous [*a*vous conduisiez comme elle.] Tachez de l'imiter. C'est ce que vous pouvez faire de mieux.*a*

SERVILIE

Imiter quelqu'un, moi! Non, mon frere, je suis originale, et je m'en pique. Moi, imiter un enfant qui fait la prude! Eh mais! vous ne songés donc pas à ce que vous dites? *a*Vous deraisonnez, mon frere, vous deraisonnez.*a*

CATON

C'est bien vous qui extravagués.

SERVILIE

Tenés, [x] je gage que nos delicieuses [*a*Saturnales ennuient Cornelie*a*] autant que vous. [*a*Vous estes fais l'un pour l'autre. En verité, mon frere, vous devriez vous*a*] amuser à en ètre amoureux, le beau couple! [*a*Ah,*a*] je vous prie, divertissés-moi *a*de cette scene. Cela seroit divin.*a*

CATON

Quel supplice d'entendre . . .

SERVILIE

Oui, il est trés douloureux [*a*d'etre temoins de la gaïeté des autres*a*]: mais il faut en passer par là.

CATON

Non, je puis m'epargner [*a*cet ennui*a*]. Adieu.

[81.18]   Scene 6ᵉ

                   Servilie, Bacchis

SERVILIE

Avoüe, Bacchis, que mon frere est bien ridicule?

BACCHIS

Il est insupportable.

SERVILIE

Point du tout, je l'aime [x] mieux de cette humeur que [*de tout autre*].

BACCHIS

Ah ah! Comment cela?

SERVILIE

C'est qu'il me divertit. S'il n'etoit que raisonnable, il m'ennuieroit à mourir. La raison est si froide, si languissante! [*Mais*] mon frere tel qu'il est me fournit tous les jours mille occasions de le contredire, de le [*metre en colere, de l'impatianter*], et cela met de la vivacité dans le commerce. On s'apperçoit que l'on vit; [*rien n'est si plaisant*].

BACCHIS

J'admire les rafinements que vous fournit le gout du plaisir. Vous en trouvés dans ce qui [*desoleroit*] une autre.

SERVILIE

Ai-je tort?

BACCHIS

Tort! Je ne dis pas cela.

SERVILIE

Tiens, Bacchis, si tu voulois me seconder, [81.19] nous désespererions mon frere.

BACCHIS

Oui, mais je paierois pour deux.

SERVILIE

Par exemple, aprés que mes amies sont sorties les soirs, si tu voulois nous passerions le reste des nuits à faire du bruit dans la [ᵃmaison, a courir, a danser et a chanter, il en deviendroit fouᵃ].

BACCHIS

Ne veillés-vous pas assés tard? Il n'en [ᵃest dejaᵃ] que trop en colere.

SERVILIE

Tant pis pour lui. Il n'est tard à [ᵃla premiere heures de la nuitᵃ] que pour les chats huants qui se couchent a [ᵃla huitieme du jourᵃ].

BACCHIS

Le patron vous passeroit encore cet article si vous emploïés ce tems à lire, à vous occuper de bonnes choses. Il me le repête tous les jours.

SERVILIE

Je le crois bien, il voudroit me rendre aussi ridicule que lui. C'est la lecture qui lui a gaté l'esprit, à lui, à Ciceron [x], enfin à tous ces ennuieux dont il fait ses delices. Oh que je n'ai garde de donner dans le piège! Je l'ai bien resolu, je ne lirai qu'en portant des lunettes, et j'en suis encore loin, comme tu vois.

[81.20]   BACCHIS

Sans doute, car vous n'en ferés usage que le plus tard que vous pourés; et cependant Caton pretend . . . ᵃmais qu'alois-je dire?ᵃ

SERVILIE

Acheve, acheve, il pretend quoi?

BACCHIS

Tenés, ma chere Maitresse, je suis si lasse de ses mauvais discours, que je ne veux pas les repeter.

SERVILIE

Conte-les-moi, Bacchis, je [*t'en conjure*]. Est-il rien de plus divertissant que les extravagances de mon frere

BACCHIS

D'abord il dit que vous ne ressemblés point à une Romaine.

SERVILIE

Ah! que cela est plaisant! [*Je voudrois bien*] savoir [x] ce que c'est que l'air d'une Romaine.

BACCHIS

[*C'est, dit-il*], un air grave, une mine serieuse un peu alongée.

SERVILIE

En faut-il d'avantage pour prouver la folie de Caton? On a la mine et l'air de son caractere. A-t'il trouvé [81.21] dans quelques vielles loix de Numa qu'il fut deffendu à une Romaine d'etre gaye?

BACCHIS

Je ne sais pas. Mais vous ètes méchante, dit-il.

SERVILIE

[*Je t'en fais juge, Bacchis.*] Ai-je jamais fait battre un esclave? Fais-je du mal à qui que ce soit?

BACCHIS

Vous ètes medisante.

SERVILIE

C'est que je suis sincere. Je dis tout ce que je pense, c'est une vertu.

BACCHIS

Eh bien! Je gage que s'il vous entendoit il vous repondroit que cette vertu poussée un peu loin est un vice. C'est Caton qui parle au moins.

SERVILIE

Et quand ce seroit toi, les Saturnales ne te [x] permettent-[*elles
pas de tout dire, et moi je te permets*] encore d'avantage. Eh bien
donc, [*parles, acheve*].

BACCHIS

Vous êtes railleuse, mordante . . .

SERVILIE

Oh pour cela, c'est un talent. Les Dieux pour me dédomager de
m'avoir fait naitre la sœur de Caton, m'ont donné une sagacité mer-
veilleuse pour pénétrer les ridicules. C'est le bonheur de ma vie.

[81.22]   BACCHIS

Et la coquetterie, est-elle aussi un présent des Dieux?

SERVILIE

Bacchis me croit coquette?

BACCHIS

Je vous ai deja dit que c'est Caton qui parle.

SERVILIE

Mais toi qu'en pense-tu?

BACCHIS

Eh! mais . . .

SERVILIE

Ah Bacchis! Si c'est être coquette que d'aimer eperdument le plus
aimable des Romains, [x] je la suis *beaucoup*.

BACCHIS

Non, ce n'est pas être coquette, c'est être mal avisée.

SERVILIE

Comment?

BACCHIS

Parce qu'il n'est rien de si malheureux pour une femme que d'aimer sans être aimée.

SERVILIE

Et quand on est adoré, Bacchis?

BACCHIS

Passe encore. [x] Auriés-vous un nouvel amant?

[81.23]   SERVILIE

Toujours le même, ma chere Bacchis, toujours le même.

BACCHIS

Qui? Cesar?

SERVILIE

Tu l'as dit.

BACCHIS

Cesar vous aime!

SERVILIE

Pourquoi cet air d'étonnement? Pourquoi ne plairois-je pas à Cesar?

BACCHIS

Parce que vous avés trop voulu lui plaire. Les hommes n'aiment pas qu'on leur fasse les avances.

SERVILIE

Mais, Bacchis, si je lui plais?

BACCHIS

Que me contez-vous là? Il y a dix ans qu'il ne pense plus à vous, encore n'y a-t'il pensé qu'un moment.

SERVILIE

Il revient, Bachis, il revient. Cesar est infidèle sans être inconstant.

BACCHIS

Je n'entends pas cette subtilité. [x]

SERVILIE

Quoi! Tu es incrédule! Ma pauvre Bacchis, que diras-tu quand tu verras Cesar?

BACCHIS

Ou?

SERVILIE

Ici dans mon appartment.

BACCHIS

Cesar dans la maison de Caton, son mortel ennemi?

[81.24]   SERVILIE

C'est ce qui doit te prouver l'excés de sa passion.

BACCHIS

J'aurois pû croire il y a dix ans que Cesar auroit tout entrepris pour vous voir; *parce que son impetuosité naturelle lui fait faire pour un gout passager les meme extravaguances qu'un autre en feroit pour une vray passion. [Mais apres dix ans. . . .*]

SERVILIE

Sais-tu bien que tu gagne la sotte façon de penser de mon frere, c'est une contagion.

[*BACCHIS

Ce n'est point humeur, c'est que je ne me fie pas a de tels amans.

SERVILIE

Et si je te montrois un billet.

BACCHIS

Un billet de Cesar?*]

135

SERVILIE

[x] Tiens, lis donc, incredule. (*Elle lui donne un billet.*)

BACCHIS

J'ai lû et je doute encore.

SERVILIE

[*ª*As-tu bien vu*ª*] avec quelle tendresse il me demande la permission de s'introduire chez mon frere à la faveur des Saturnales, d'y passer la journée déguisé en esclave? Cesar en esclave! Ce pauvre enfant! Quel sacrifice! Quelle preuve d'amour! Je suis ravie, enchantée . . .

BACCHIS

Eh! Moderés-vous donc.

SERVILIE

De la moderation à moi. [*ª*Adieu.*ª*] Je cours repondre à ce charmant, à cet adorable billet.

Fin du 1ᵉʳ acte.

[81.25]   ACTE 2ᵉ

Scene 1ʳᵉ

Cornelie, Sostrata

CORNELIE

Eloignons-nous, je vous prie, ma chere Sostrata, cette fête tumul-
tueuse n'a rien qui me plaise. Je vous prive peut-être d'un spectacle
qui vous est agréable; mais je vous tiendrai compte du sacrifice.

SOSTRATA

Ce qui peut plaire à ma chere maitresse ne sera jamais un sacrifice.

CORNELIE

Quelle fête orageuse! Quel bruit! On l'appelle la fête de la liberté,
j'ai cru la liberté plus tranquile.

SOSTRATA

C'est que vous ne connoissés que celle des honnêtes gens. Ils y
sont accoutumés, ils en jouissent sans s'en appercevoir. Mais la liberté
de ces miserables qui revient rarement, et qui ne dure que quelques
jours leur inspire des transports de joie qui produisent ce que vous
entendés.

CORNELIE

Helas! Je ne condamne point ces pauvres esclaves. Ils ont si peu de
tems à se divertir qu'il est bien juste qu'ils en profitent. Mais ce qui
m'etonne c'est que des citoiens se mêlent à leurs jeux.

SOSTRATA

Servilie par exemple: qu'a-t'elle affaire [81.26] à tous ces gens là.
Leur plaisir lui devroit etre tout à fait etranger.

137

CORNELIE

Ce n'etoit point elle à qui je pensois, Sostrata. Servilie est née avec du penchant [*a la gaieté. Elle n'est point condamnable.*] Si j'étois de la même humeur, je ferois comme elle.

SOSTRATA

Vous iriés, comme je viens de la voir, vous mettre à la tête de tous ces fous danser et crier comme eux? *Car rien ne la distingue de la foule que la magnificence de ses habillements.*

CORNELIE

Eh! mais . . . peut-être . . .

SOSTRATA

Et vous pousseriés, comme elle, la coquetterie et l'envie de plaire depuis Cesar jusqu'aux esclaves? Car à son air, à ses manieres, on diroit qu'elle veut pour amant tout ce qui l'environne.

CORNELIE

Arretés, Sostrate, elle est sœur de Caton, d'un ami de mon pere, nous devons la respecter.

SOSTRATA

Tenés, madame, pour attirer le respect des autres, il faut se respecter soi même.

CORNELIE

Eh bien! puisque vous savés cela, respectés-vous donc assés pour ne [*blamer*] personne.

SOSTRATA

[*Coment, il n'est pas permis . . .*]

[81.27] CORNELIE

Non, comptés, Sostrata, que la médisance fait plus de tort aux femmes que leur conduite; et que si elles se plaisoient moins à relever

138

reciproquement leurs deffauts, et même à les grossir, on les respecteroit d'avantage.

SOSTRATA

Par Junon! Ceux de Servilie sautent si fort aux yeux qu'il est impossible de s'en taire.

CORNELIE

Mais si Bacchis s'entretenoit des miens avec [ᵃsa maitresseᵃ], vous m'aimés assés pour en ètre offensée, j'en suis sure. Pourquoi voulés-vous me parler [x] de ceux de Servilie? Il faut ètre juste.

SOSTRATA

Eh pardi! Ma chere Patrone, je les mets au pis. Qu'elles disent vos deffauts, et je dirai les leurs, nous verrons qui parlera plus longtems.

CORNELIE

Vous n'y gagneriés pas beaucoup. Si mes deffauts different de ceux de Servilie, je n'en ai peutêtre pas moins, et vous me voiés d'assés près pour les connoitre.

SOSTRATA

Non, je ne vous connois que des ridicules. [ᵃPar exemple,ᵃ] à votre âge, vous ètes modeste, réservée comme une Romaine du tems des Scipions et des Camilles? Oh! cela n'est pas supportable dans ce siècle-ci.

CORNELIE

Vous me conseilleriés donc de changer de conduite?

[81.28]   SOSTRATA

Oh! que non, je ne suis pas si sotte, je n'ai point envie de changer de maitresse. Helas! ou trouverois-je une aussi bonne, aussi vertueuse, aussi parfaite?

CORNELIE

Sostrata, vous ne me croiés pas si parfaite, puisque vous me loués à cet excés.

SOSTRATA

Excusés-moi, s'il vous plait, je n'entends pas ce que vous voulés dire.

CORNELIE

Si vous croiés que vos louanges me plaisent, vous [*pensez*] donc que j'aime la flatterie, et assurément [*ce seroit*] un grand deffaut.

SOSTRATA

Belle consequence! Je ne l'aurois jamais deviné. Non non, je suis bien loin de vous croire ce gout-là. Mais encore faut-il me donner quelquefois la licence de vous dire vos verités, les Saturnales me le permettent.

CORNELIE

Eh bien! cette nouvelle tournure que vous prenés pour dire les mêmes choses n'est-elle pas encore plus dangereuse que la premiere?

SOSTRATA

Ma foi! on ne saura bientot plus comment vous parler. Voulés-vous que je vous dise que vous etes fausse, méchante, coquette, étourdie? Je vous déplairois encore, car vous haïssés le mensonge et la calomnie. [81.29] [x]

CORNELIE

Rien n'est si aisé, ma chere Sostrata; il n'y a qu'à ne parler de moi que pour m'avertir de mes fautes.

SOSTRATA

Vous ne m'y resoudrés jamais. Tout ce qui me frappe excite en moi l'envie de parler. Je vois vos vertus, je ne saurois m'en taire. Eh bien! supposés que c'est mon deffaut, vous ètes indulgente, passés-le moi.

CORNELIE

En verité, Sostrata, je crains de m'accoutumer à vos flatteries, ce seroit un grand malheur.

SOSTRATA

Comment donc? J'en frémis pour vous.

CORNELIE

Ne raillés pas, rien n'est si dangereux.

SOSTRATA

D'accord, mais parlons serieusement. Savés-vous bien qu'il ne faut pas tant ignorer ce que l'on vaut, et que cela peut décourager.

CORNELIE

Mais aussi . . .

SOSTRATA

Il n'y a point de mais aussi là dedans. Rien ne donne tant d'envie d'atteindre à la perfection que d'etre bien persuadé que l'on en est fort prés.

CORNELIE

Vous m'embarassés. Il me semble cependant qu'il est aussi dangereux d'entendre dire du bien de soi que du mal des autres.

SOSTRATA

Il me semble! Craindre de se tromper en disant les meilleures choses! Voulés-vous encore que [81.30] je me taise sur cette modestie rare, singuliere, unique? Tenés, ma chere maitresse, vous ètes adorable, et s'il étoit permis à votre esclave de vous manquer de respect, je vous embrasserois.

CORNELIE

Embrassés-moi, Sostrata. Une marque d'affection n'est point un manque de respect.

SOSTRATA

Quelle bonté! Ô Cesar! Quel bonheur vous attend.

CORNELIE

N'étions-nous pas convenues que vous ne me parleriés plus de Cesar.

SOSTRATA

Oui, mais son nom est si doux à prononcer, il rapelle l'idée d'un Romain si aimable, qu'il m'echape sans y penser.

CORNELIE

Vous n'étes pas sincere, Sostrata; et ce détour est maladroit.

SOSTRATA

En verité on est toujours embarassé quand on vous parle. Vous fuiés le monde, vous me permettés de vous entretenir, et tous mes discours vous déplaisent. Quelle est la jeune personne qui ne trouve pas du plaisir à entendre parler de son amant.

CORNELIE

Je n'ai point d'amant, et je ne dois point en avoir.

SOSTRATA

Oh pour le coup! Ceci passe le but, et vous tombés dans la pruderie. Cesar n'a-t'il pas [81.31] la parole de votre pere? Ne doit-il pas dans trés peu de tems devenir votre epoux?

CORNELIE

Il peut devenir mon epoux sans ètre mon amant.

SOSTRATA

Je m'y perds. Cesar vous adore, aucune femme n'a pû le fixer jusqu'ici. Fiancé à . . .² il la rend à ses parents pour n'étre attaché qu'à vous. Jamais passion ne parut si vive et si constante. Que faut-il donc pour ètre amant?

---

² the name of César's fiancée was left blank in the manuscript.

CORNELIE

Ce mot semble supposer qu'un homme est aimé, c'est en quoi il me blesse.

SOSTRATA

Et quand cela seroit? Le grand malheur! Je ne vous demande pas [ªde m'avouer que vous aimez Cesar, ceª] seroit peine perdue. Mais je diminuerois beaucoup de mon estime pour vous, si vous [ªne l'aimiés pasª].

CORNELIE

Pourquoi?

SOSTRATA

Parceque vous me montreriés de la dissimulation, ou une pruderie ridicule. Tout ce qui peut engager une fille à aimer se rencontre dans Cesar, les charmes de la personne, son mérite, sa noblesse, sa grandeur future, son amour present, et ce qui couronne tout cela, l'aveu de votre pere.

CORNELIE

[ªEh bien, Sostrata, il faut donc l'avouer.ª] Je ne perdrai rien de votre estime.

[81.32]   SOSTRATA

Ah! ma chere maitresse, que votre confiance m'honnore! Elle me comble de joie.

CORNELIE

Si vous en abusiés, [x] je serois ªbienª malheureuse, mais voici encore des esclaves, ils nous poursuivent jusqu'ici. Retirons-nous.

SOSTRATA

Que vois-je? Madame, madame, revenés, je ne sais si je me trompe; mais ceux-ci me paroissent de meilleure compagnie que les autres.

143

Scene 2ᵉ

Cornelie, Sostrata, Cesar, Cratinus

CESAR *à Cratinus*

C'est elle, retire-toi. Vas faire executer mes ordres, et reviens avec les [ᵃpresensᵃ].

CORNELIE

Ô Dieux! Cesar! Cesar en ces lieux!

CESAR

Oui, belle Cornelie, désesperé de votre éloignement j'ose tout entreprendre pour jouir d'un moment de votre vue.

CORNELIE

Quoi! Cesar ne dedaigne pas de s'abaisser jusqu'à ce vile déguisement! J'aurois cru que toutes ses actions devoient avoir l'eclat, [ᵃetᵃ] la grandeur qu'il affecte dans ses desseins.

CESAR

Cesar à vos pieds est l'esclave le plus soumis, par tout ailleurs il ne connoit point d'egal. Dans Rome tout à la gloire, auprés de vous tout à l'amour . . .

[81.33]   CORNELIE

Cesar, ne sortés point du respect qui m'est dû. Me parler de votre amour, c'est en manquer.

CESAR

Eh quoi! Belle Cornelie, l'aveu de votre pere ne suffit-il pas pour autoriser mes sentimens et rassurer votre vertu?

CORNELIE

J'ignore ce que mon pere vous a promis, mais il ne m'a point ordonné de vous entendre.

CESAR

Eh quoi! La fille de Cinna veut ignorer les engagements de son pere afin de me montrer plus de dédains.

CORNELIE

Si l'intention de mon pere eut eté de vous permettre de me voir pendant son absence, il ne m'auroit pas confiée à Caton. La maison de votre ennemi doit vous ètre interdite.

CESAR

Si Caton est mon ennemi, je ne suis pas le sien. Votre pere connoit nos differents; pensés-vous, Cornelie, qu'il m'accordât sa bienveillance s'il avoit pour moi aussi peu d'estime que vous m'en temoignés. "Non, non, il sait trop que la haine de Caton est injuste."

CORNELIE

["J'en ignore la cause"]; mais il a trop de vertu pour qu'elle ne soit pas legitime. C'est un Romain si grand, si vertueux, que jusqu'à sa haine tout "devroit en lui vous paroitre respectable."

[81.34]   CESAR

Ah! C'est pousser trop loin le mépris! L'amour, belle Cornelie, me fera supporter tout celui dont vous voudrés m'accabler, quand il n'aura de rapport qu'a vous. Mais si vous me comparés à Caton, si vous me croiés assés lache pour ètre humilié de la haine d'un Cinique, dont l'orgueil farouche emprunte pour s'honnorer, le langage de la liberté, c'est un outrage si cruel que Cesar se croiroit indigne de la main de Cornelie s'il étoit capable de le supporter.

SOSTRATA

Finissés aussi, vous le mettés au desespoir.

CORNELIE

Je n'ai point pretendu vous offenser, Cesar. J'avoue que l'austérité des vertus de Caton . . .

CESAR

devroit vous les faire hair. Elles cessent d'être vertus dès qu'elles sont effraiantes. La véritable vertu vous ressemble belle Cornelie, elle a tous vos charmes, on ne la voit point sans l'adorer.

SOSTRATA

Qu'il est aimable!

CORNELIE

Cesar sait tout rassembler. La galanterie se mêle à ses discours les plus serieux. Mais [ᵃces discours subtils ne prouvent rien contre Caton. Il sera toujours louable de deffendreᵃ] la liberté romaine que vous voulés opprimer.
[81.35] [blank]³

[81.36]   ᵃCESAR

Eh de grace, madame, montrez moins de mepris pour moi et ne me croiez pas asses lache pour respecter la haine d'un cinique dont l'orgueil farouche declame contre les vices par mepris pour les hommes et qui ne connoit de vertus que celles qui font haïr, et qui peutetre seroit resté dans l'oubli et le dernier citoien de Rome s'il ne craignoit que je n'en devinsses le premier.

CORNELIE

Cesar, montrez plus de moderation contre un sage. . . .

CESAR

Il abuse, madame, de celle que j'ai gardé jusqu'ici, et si j'etois aussi injuste que Caton il se repentirois bientot . . .

CORNELIE

Quoi, des menaces dans sa propre maison!

CESAR

Non, madame, il n'arrivera jamais a Caton que le mal qu'il voudra se faire. Je lui donnerai toujours des exemples de generosité, qu'il ne

³ pp.35-36 are an extra sheet, meant to replace the text from the top of p.34 down to Cornelie's last speech.

suivra pas, de moderation qui ne le toucheront pas. Enfin je forcerai l'univers a convenir que Cesar etoit aussi vertueux que Caton etoit inflexible.

CORNELIE

Vous ne pouvez au moins blamer ses intentions. Il voudroit donner a la vertu l'empire sur les cœurs.

CESAR

Est-ce donc en la montrant dure, arrogante, inflexible, meprisante, qu'on peut la faire aimer? Non, belle Cornelie, la vertu doit vous ressembler. Qu'on la presente noble, douce, magnanime, enfin avec tous vos charmes. Les mortels se disputeront la gloire de l'adorer.

CORNELIE*

[81.37]   CESAR

Vous ignorés, Cornelie, et vous devés ignorer ce que c'est que cette prétendue liberté. Votre pere quatre fois Consul connoit les intérets de Rome, et ne me blame pas. Elle ne peut ètre sauvée du desordre et du brigandage de ses citoiens que par un seul maître. Et si j'aspire à l'ètre mes intentions sont plus droites que celles de Caton [*en s'opposant a moi*].

CORNELIE

Mais le dessein de subjuguer sa patrie a toujours quelque chose d'odieux.

CESAR

Oui, madame, quand le courage et l'honneur ne soutiennent pas l'ambition. Je veux rendre a ma Patrie son ancienne splendeur ensevelie sous la brigue de l'intérêt et de la bassesse. Je veux relever l'eclat du nom Romain, et que ma gloire soit la sienne. [*Si la belle*] Cornelie daigne la partager, il ne restera à l'heureux Cesar aucuns voeux à faire. [xxx 2 lines]

CORNELIE

C'est a la volonté de mon pere [*a decider. Ce n'est*] point à moi à connoitre celui qui sera digne ou non d'etre mon epoux.

CESAR

Quelle indifference outrageante! quoi, [81.38] madame! que votre pere vous choisisse pour epoux Cesar ou le lâche Didius, votre obeissance seroit égale?

CORNELIE

L'obeissance est le plus cher et le plus sacré de mes devoirs.

CESAR

Ah Cornelie! Par les Dieux, par vous même, je vous conjure à genoux de ne point me laisser dans le desespoir ou me jette une indifference si remplie de mépris.

CORNELIE

Qu'osés-vous faire? Cesar, ne me faites point repentir de trop de complaisance. Je vous ai permis de me parler, je vous ai repondu; peut-être je ne devois faire ni l'un ni l'autre.

CESAR

Oui, cruelle, repentés-vous de m'avoir parlé, mais repentés-vous en même tems des outrages dont vous m'avés accablé. Je vous suis odieux, je le vois, je le sais, mais les effets de mon desespoir vous feront connoitre que je n'etois pas indigne de votre estime.

SOSTRATA

Dites-lui donc un mot qui le console.

CORNELIE

Cesar, il suffit que vous soiés ami de mon pere pour que je vous accorde mon [81.39] estime, et je ne crois pas vous avoir montré d'autres sentiments.

CESAR

Achevés, belle Cornelie, rendés le calme à mon ame. Dites-moi seulement que ce sera sans repugnance que . . .

CORNELIE

Je vous l'ai dit, j'obeirai quand mon pere parlera. ªAdieu.ª

CESAR

Ah de grace, un moment.

CORNELIE

Non, je ne puis vous écouter plus longtems. Sortés de la maison de Caton, ne l'insultés pas d'avantage par cette licence.

CESAR

Il ne me connoitra pas, les Saturnales autorisent mon déguisement. Souffrés ...

CORNELIE

Je vous ai fait connoitre ce que je desire, je n'ai rien à y ajouter.

CESAR

Encore un mot.

SOSTRATA

Ne l'obstinés pas, je lui parlerai. Voilà votre affranchi qui vous cherche, elle [ᵃcraintᵃ] les témoins.

Scene 3ᵉ

Cesar, Cratinus

CRATINUS

Les presents seront ici dans un moment.

CESAR

Ah Cratinus!

CRATINUS

Par Venus! Je crois que vous soupirés?

[81.40]   CESAR

Oui Cratinus, tu vois Cesar humilié pour la premiere fois par l'amour.

CRATINUS

Il y a cependant longtems que vous lui rendés hommage.

CESAR

Je n'aimois point, Cratinus! L'inconstance qu'on me reproche étoit plutot un amusement de l'esprit qu'un deffaut du cœur. Il étoit reservé à Cornelie de [*ᵃ*soumettre le volage Cesar*ᵃ*].

CRATINUS

Elle est belle, [*ᵃ*en effet*ᵃ*].

CESAR

Sa beauté a la moindre part à son triomphe. [x] Tu ne conçois pas le plaisir enchanteur que j'aurois à soumettre une ame toute Romaine. La fille de Cinna rassemble en elle une fierté sans orgueil, une douceur majestueuse, une décence sans affectation que l'on ne trouve plus parmi nos femmes d'aujourdhui.

CRATINUS

Ah! voilà ce qui vous pique, mon cher Patron. La coquetterie n'a qu'un tems, une beauté vient qui vange les autres. Mais à propos de coquetterie: j'ai fait rendre votre billet à la sœur de Caton. [*ᵃ*Savez vous bien qu'il*ᵃ*] y a conscience à réveiller dans cette pauvre creature une folie que peut-être elle [*ᵃ*avoit*ᵃ*] oubliée.

CESAR

Eh! pouvois-je autrement m'introduire dans la maison de Caton? Il falloit bien que Servilie se crut l'objet de mon déguisement. Elle est vindicative; si elle [*ᵃ*avoit pu*ᵃ*] soupçonner que Cornelie . . . cette pensée me fait frémir.

[81.41]   CRATINUS

[*ᵃ*Bon. bon! Des que vous lui parlerez*ᵃ*] elle croira tout ce que vous voudrés.

CESAR

Oui, mais je voudrois eviter sa rencontre.

CRATINUS

Ah! tout au moins . . .

CESAR

Non, je ne puis me resoudre à me preter à son extravagance.

CRATINUS

Vous ètes devenu furieusement délicat.

CESAR

C'est l'effet de l'amour sincere. Il rend vertueux, [x] je l'éprouve. Mais ne perdons point un tems qui pouroit attirer Servilie dans ce vestibule. Je vais chercher quelqu'endroit ou je puisse me soustraire à ses récherches.

CRATINUS

Il seroit bien plus simple de sortir de la maison. Vous avés parlé à Cornelie, c'est ce que vous vouliés. Allons.

CESAR

Non, j'ai de bons avis que Cinna revient ce soir, je veux l'attendre. S'il consulte Caton sur son engagement avec moi, il l'obligera à le rompre. Je veux le prévenir, [ªet d'alieurs mon impatienceª] ne me permet pas de differer.

CRATINUS

Et moi, que ferai-je?

CESAR

Demeures-ici, attends les porteurs de presents, presentes-les à Servilie, puisqu'enfin il faut qu'ils passent par elle. Mais surtout emploie toute ton adresse à lui persuader d'en faire part à Cornelie, [ªdªª] engager cette fiere beauté à ètre temoin de l'espèce de fête dont les [81.42] presents seront accompagnés.

CRATINUS

La commission n'est pas aisée.

151

CESAR

Ces prétendus Esclaves sont bien instruits. Tu n'as rien épargné pour leurs habillements?

CRATINUS

Eh! non, je n'ai que trop dépensé.

CESAR

Au reste que Servilie ne voie dans les conseils que tu lui donneras qu'une simple attention de ma part pour la fille d'un de nos premiers magistrats, que je suppose ètre son amie. Point de maladresse, Cratinus, point d'indiscretion.

CRATINUS

Soiés en repos, tout ira bien.

Scene 4e

CRATINUS

Il s'en faut peu que je ne plaigne cette pauvre Servilie. Quel homme que mon Patron! La force, la legereté, la galanterie, la politique, les amusements frivoles, et les desseins les plus vastes, il reunit tout, il possede tout, il a le merite superieur de chaque chose. On diroit qu'il a plusieurs ames, et que toutes sont eminentes. Servilie a le gout bon, il en faut convenir, mais malheureusement elle a précédé Cesar dans le monde de dix ou douze ans, c'est un tort irréparable. Mais la voici, elle ne m'a pas vû, ecoutons un moment pour prendre langue.

[81.43]   Scene 5e

Cratinus, Servilie, Bacchis

BACCHIS

Mais ou voulés-vous donc aller, madame? Vous parcourés toute la maison d'une telle rapidité que j'ai peine à vous suivre.

SERVILIE

Je veux trouver quelqu'un pour faire rendre ce billet à Cesar.

BACCHIS

Eh! faut-il aller si loin? Envoiés un de vos esclaves.

SERVILIE

Non, non, mon frere le sauroit. D'ailleurs je connois Cesar toujours attentif, *toujours empressé.* Je suis sure que quelqu'un de sa part est ici qui attend ma reponse.

CRATINUS

Rien n'est plus certain, madame, je suis pret à recevoir vos ordres.

SERVILIE

Eh bien! L'avois-je dit? Tenés, Cratinus, courés, volés à Cesar. Chaque moment retarde le plaisir que j'aurai à le voir.

CRATINUS

Il faut cependant que je reste encore un moment ici.

SERVILIE

L'attendriés-vous? Viendroit-il [*lui meme me surprendre? Que cet empressement, que cette indiscretion seroit aimable! Ah je lui pardonne, je lui pardonne*].

BACCHIS

Oh! oui, nous ne sommes pas difficiles sur [*le ceremonial. Nous voulons bien que l'on nous surprene agreablement*].

[81.44] SERVILIE

Cela marque [*une vivassité de sentiment toujours flatteuse*].

CRATINUS

Oui, madame, mais le respect retient.

SERVILIE

[x] Si vous n'attendés point Cesar, qui vous arrête? ᵃPartez donc.ᵃ

CRATINUS

Ses ordres, madame. Je dois vous présenter des présents qui le devançent. Vous ne pouvés les refuser dans un tems qui permet même aux esclaves d'en faire à leur Maitre.

SERVILIE

[ᵃDes presens, Bacchis, des presens! Doutes-tu encore? Que faut-il pour te persuader. Cesar pense a tout, il n'oublie rien. Il profite de toutes les libertés que donne la fete. Mais Cratinus, il faut que je sois aimée etonnement.ᵃ]

CRATINUS

ᵃAh madame,ᵃ cela ne se comprend pas. Et vous l'aimés de même sans doute?

SERVILIE

Oh! comme vous dites, cela ne se conçoit pas. [x] Dites-moi, Cratinus: étoit-il dejà déguisé quand il vous a envoié ici? [ᵃAh je n'en doute pas, son impatiance ne lui a pas permis d'attendreᵃ] mon billet. [ᵃIl estᵃ] toujours beau, toujours charmant sous cet habit d'esclave? [ᵃOh oui, j'en suis sure. Parlez doncᵃ], repondés donc. [x]

BACCHIS

Que Minerve vous aide, ma chere maitresse! [ᵃHelasᵃ], vous extravagués. [ᵃQue voulez-vous qu'on vous reponde? Vous repondez vous meme.ᵃ]

[81.45]   CRATINUS

Que tu es pauvre d'esprit, Bacchis? [ᵃsi tu crois qu'il ne me reste rien a dire. Oui, madame, Cesarᵃ] sous l'habit d'esclave est à ravir. Il y conserve cet air de maitre du monde qu'on lui a toujours remarqué, et qu'il semble que les Dieux aient imprimé sur son front.

SERVILIE

Eh bien, Bacchis? Eh bien?

BACCHIS

Eh bien, madame! Cesar est toujours beau, et Cratinus un fripon, ["ou je me trompe fort"].

CRATINUS

Ah! Voici nos gens.

Scene 6ᵉ

Servilie, Bacchis, Cratinus

Une troupe de danseurs déguisés en esclaves mettent les présents aux pieds de Servilie en dansant.

SERVILIE

Quelle magnificence! Quelle profusion! Bacchis, vois-tu tout l'amour de Cesar dans cette galanterie?

CRATINUS

Ô vous ne voiés pas, madame, jusqu'ou Cesar porte les attentions. La moitié de ces bijoux et de ces étoffes sont pour Cornelie.

BACCHIS

Haye haye!

SERVILIE

Et pourquoi pour Cornelie? Que voulés-vous dire? Que pense Cesar?

[81.46]   **CRATINUS**

Il pense que vous protegés cette petite fille.

SERVILIE

Moi? Point du tout.

CRATINUS

Et qu'il vous prouve son amour en étendant ses galanteries jusqu'à elle.

SERVILIE

Cela est fort mal pensé.

CRATINUS

D'ailleurs que sait-on? Peut-être il est bien aise de gagner Cinna. C'est un homme puissant dans la République; et [*d'alieurs je me crois obligé de vous avertir en confidence que Cesar a le foible de n'aimer*] point à voir contrarier ses projets, [x] cependant vous ètes la [*maitresse d'en user comme il vous plaira*]. Voiés aussi des presents pour Bacchis et pour Sostrata.

SERVILIE

Il me vient une idée. Oui oui, la fille de Cinna partagera ces presents. [*Cela me donnera un grand avantage sur elle. Je veux la voir secher de depit en me voiant un amant tel que Cesar.

CRATINUS

C'est fort bien fait.

SERVILIE

Il me vient une autre idée. J'en veux aussi donner a mon frere. Il sera furieux et cela sera tres plaisant. Bacchis, fais porter ces etoffes dans son appartement apres que tu auras distribué cet argent a ces esclaves. Vous, Cratinus, courez, volez, portez ma reponce a Cesar, et que ses esclaves me divertissent en attendant par leur danses.

(*Bacchis donne l'argent aux esclaves qui le recoivent*] *en dansant, ce qui forme le ballet.*)

Fin du 2ᵉ acte.

　　　　　　　ACTE 3^e

Scene 1re

CATON

Partout ou j'ai porté mes pas la joie effrenée me poursuit, elle ouvre
des precipices qui peuvent ensevelir la patrie et la liberté. Ô Rome!
c'est peut-être au milieu de tes fêtes que ton peril est le plus grand.
Tout le monde blame ma defiance, l'ennivrement est general, personne
ne veut prévoir le danger. [*J'ai cependant de bons avis*] que Cesar
est sorti de chez lui déguisé en esclave. Quel dessein a pû le porter à
cette bassesse? Il faut absolument que je le pénètre. La confusion est si
grande qu'elle a mis la vigilance de mes espions en deffaut, ils n'ont pû
le suivre. Dromon est le seul qui ne soit point encore rentré. Peut-être
[*il en saura davantage*]. Le voici.

Scene 2^e

Caton, Dromon

CATON

Eh bien Dromon! Que viens-tu m'apprendre?

DROMON

Que Rome est en feu.

CATON

Ah! Je l'avois prévû! Lâches amis! Vous n'avés pas voulus me croire,
mais vous perirés ainsique moi.

　　　　　　DROMON

Par Jupiter! Si vos amis perissent, ce sera au moins d'une mort gaie.
Je les ai trouvé et laissé de la plus belle humeur du monde. Ils vous
invitent à faire comme eux, c'est toute la reponse que j'en ai tirée.

CATON

L'effroi leur a donc oté la raison?

DROMON

L'effroi! Eh! De quoi voulés-vous qu'il s'effraient?

CATON

Comment! Pour porter l'allarme dans leur ame insensible [*faut-il*]
attendre que Rome soit réduite en cendre. *On ne songe donc pas a la
secourir.*

DROMON

En voici bien d'une autre! Quoi! Vous croiés que Rome va perir?

CATON

Ne m'as-tu pas dit qu'elle étoit en feu?

DROMON

Oui, mais je parlois de celui des illuminations qui font un effet
admirable, et [*qui raniment la joye et les clameurs du peuple. On
n'entendroit pas bien tonner*].

CATON

Seroit-il possible qu'en effet . . .

DROMON

[*Allés-vous*] douter d'une chose toute naturelle, afin de ne pas
perdre le chagrin dont vous vous regaliés dejà sur un malheur imagi-
naire! Vous ètes, il faut l'avouer, bien ingénieux à vous tourmenter.

CATON

L'interet de ma patrie m'occupe tout entier et quand tu me dis
que Rome est en feu, comment veux-tu que je devine que ce sont des
illuminations?

[81.49] DROMON

En effet cela étoit fort difficile à trouver. Cette magnificence ne fait-elle pas un acte de religion des Saturnales? Mais vous ne voiés rien qu'en noir, et votre maison vous ressemble. Elle est la seule dans Rome qui ne soit pas eclairée. Mais par Saturne! Je vais y mettre bon ordre.

CATON

Arrète. Rends-moi compte de ce que tu as appris?

DROMON

Non, cela vous chagrineroit encore.

CATON

Parle, je le veux.

DROMON

Ne soiés point curieux, croiés-moi.

CATON

Quoi, malheureux! Tu trahirois [*la republique*] en me cachant les malheurs qu'on lui prépare?

DROMON

Non, je ne dirai rien à moins que vous ne me promettiés de ne vous point mettre en colere.

CATON

Finiras-tu, miserable? Tu redoubles mon impatience.

DROMON

Doucement, *puisque vous le voulez,* vous allés tout savoir. Eh bien, mon cher Patron! Dans les courses que vous [*m'avez fait faire j'ai apris

CATON

Quoi? Parle vite.

DROMON

J'ai apris mille façons, jeu nouveaux, mille façons de me divertir

159

que j'ignorois auparavent. Tenez, l'esclave du moindre citoien*] en sait là dessus plus que *tous* les vôtres ensemble.

[81.50]   [*CATON

Miserable, tu n'es occupé que de tes plates railleries et je suis sur que tu n'as pas executé mes ordres.

DROMON

Oh que pardonnez-moi. Ne m'avez-vous pas ordonné de voir, d'examiner s'il ne se formoit pas des complots par ci par là?

CATON

Oui. Eh bien?

DROMON

Eh bien j'en ai vu de toute part.

CATON

Eh, parles donc. Il faut t'arracher les parolles.

DROMON

D'abort, toutes les places publiques sont rempliees de peuples atroupé par peloton. Ici les plus grands alongent le col pour eccouter plus attentivement par dessus la tete des autres, ce que disent deux ou trois des plus hupés qui ouvrent les avis, et la . . .

CATON

O ma chere patrie, Caton ne poura-t-il prevenir ta perte? Suis-moi, Dromon, tu as du cœur. Courons dissiper ces funestes assemblées.

DROMON

Ci ce n'est que pour cela vous pouvez rester. Elles se dissipent d'elle meme. Chaqu'un se prend par la main et la troupe s'eparpille en chantant ou en dansant suivant le resultat du complot.

CATON

Quoi, c'est pour le plaisir . . .

DROMON

Sans doute. Et je vous assure qu'a present il n'y a dans Rome aucune autre occupation. Je savois bien que j'alois vous chagriner. Vous voila tout pensif.

CATON

Il est cependant certain que Cesar est sorti de chez lui deguisé en esclave.ª]

DROMON

Eh bien! Oui, Cesar est déguisé en esclave. Voilà une chose bien intéressante pour la république!

CATON

Plus qu'on ne pense. Il n'est point de formes qu'il ne prenne pour séduire le peuple.

DROMON

Ou plutot les femmes. Allés, allés, mon cher Patron, laissés-le faire, cela ne vous regarde pas.

CATON

Je ne suis que trop instruit de ses pernicieux desseins.

DROMON

Ne voilà-t-il pas encore vos inquiétudes [81.51] mal placées? Voions; quand il prétendroit à gouverner la République, quel grand mal y auroit-il à cela?

CATON

Traitre! Tu approuve les projets de ce jeune audacieux. Ton sang ne suffiroit pas à laver un tel crime.

DROMON

Ah! Je sais que le merite de Cesar est l'ecueil de votre raison, mais reprenons un peu de sang froid. Vous ne pouvés me nier [ªque les hommes n'ayent besoin deª] loix pour [ªlesª] conduire?

CATON

Sans doute.

DROMON

Vous conviendrés aussi que celles de Rome sont mal observées?

CATON

C'est ce qui me desespere.

DROMON

Je vous entends tous les jours déclamer contre le senat, parce que, dites-vous, il est composé de trop de monde, que les passions des uns contrarient les vertus des autres, sèment la discorde entre eux, et que le bien public en souffre.

CATON

Il n'est que trop vrai.

DROMON

Je vous tiens, mon cher Patron. Car il est clair qu'un seul homme a moins de passions que cent, il n'y a qu'à compter; donc il fera moins de mal, donc il [81.52] gouvernera mieux; [x] ses vertus n'étant point contrariées, le peuple jouira du bien [*qu'elles pourront produire, et vive un seul*] maitre des Romains!

CATON

Monstre! Qu'ose-tu prononcer?

DROMON

Vous aurés beau faire l'enragé, Cesar l'emportera, je le prédis; ses vertus sont nobles, il aime les hommes, il en fait cas, il fera des heureux.

CATON

Ah! La fureur me transporte. Il vaut mieux sortir que de commettre un crime contre les loix de cette [*pernicieuse*] fête. [x] Elle finira, [*traitre, elle finira*].

162

DROMON

J'ai pris mes précautions, je ne vous crains guère.

Scene 3ᵉ

Caton, Dromon, Servilie, Bacchis

SERVILIE

Ou allés-vous donc, mon frere? Comme vous [ᵃvoila effarouché. Je gage que quelque mal intentioné vous aura fait des presens et cela vous fache, n'est-il pas vray?

CATON

Ah, vous m'en faites souvenir fort a propos. Si je savois qui de vous autres a facilité cette impertinence je l'en ferois repentir.

DROMON (*a Bacchis*)

Que veut-il dire?

BACCHIS (*bas*)

Rien. C'est un tour de ma maitresse.

SERVILIE

Vous voila donc bien faché, mon tres cher frere.

BACCHIS

Le patron a raison, madame. Quand on reçois il faut rendre et rien ne donne tant de chagrin.

[81.53]   CATON

En tout cas celui que j'en ressens ne sera pas long. Je veux que dans le moment on reporte tout a l'inpertinen qui m'a joué ce tour là. De riches etoffes a Caton! qui meprise le luxe le moins recherché. Qui peut etre l'insensé . . .

SERVILIE

Il ne tiendroit qu'a moi de vous le dire, mais je n'en ferai rien.

163

CATON

Vous savez qui m'a fait ces presens.

SERVILIE

Assurement.

CATON

Tant mieux. Mon embaras cesse. Bacchis, je vous ordonne de les renvoier tout a l'heure.

DROMON

Et moi je lui deffend. Outre que cette obeissance seroit contre nos droits, c'est qu'il faut bien vous obliger de pratiquer une fois dans votre vie la plus noble des vertus, la liberalité. C'est celle qui vous coute le plus, j'en conviens, mais aussi vous en aurez plus de merite. Alons, de l'argent.

CATON

Pour quoi faire?

DROMON

Pour aller acheter quelques bijoux rare, precieux, et les renvoier en echange des etoffes.

SERVILIE

En verité Dromon est admirable. Je ne connoissois pas tout son merite. Tiens, prends cette bource, c'est la recompense des bons avis que tu donnes a Caton. Voiez, mon frere, a quel point je vous aime.

CATON

Alez, vous etes folle. A-t-on jamais comis de tels exes! Donner de l'argent a un esclave. Vous serez responsable du mauvais usage qu'il en fera.

SERVILIE

Que m'inporte. Je donne pour moi pour avoir la satisfaction de bien faire. Tant pis pour Dromon s'il use mal de mon bienfait.

[81.54]

BACCHIS

Voila ce qui s'apelle obeir aux dieux en bonne Romaine.

CATON

Ames viles, vos dieux sont l'interet et vous prophanez leur nom en les faisant servir a votre cupidité.

BACCHIS

Et moi je vous soutiens que ce sont les dieux qui ont etablit l'usage de faire des liberalités dans cette saison afin de lier les humains par la reconnoissance et retrasser l'image de la sainte amitié qui regnoit entre les premiers hommes.

SERVILIE

Eccoutez, eccoutez Bacchis, mon frere: elle raisonne comme un pontife. Ce sont les dieux qui ordonnent de faire des presens aux hommes.

CATON

Si cela etoit vray dans les tems reculés, c'est que les hommes etoient bons et sages. A present ils sont trop mechants.[a]]

BACCHIS

Bon prétexte pour la ladrerie.

DROMON

Patron, Patron, repondés mieux, votre honneur m'est cher, je ne voudrois pas que des femmes prissent de l'avantage sur vous, et vous leur en donnés furieusement.

CATON

Que veux-tu dire?

DROMON

Le voici. Les Dieux sans contredit savent mieux que vous si les hommes sont méchants. Voiés-vous pour cela qu'ils retirent leurs bienfaits? Leur bonté se plait à les verser sur les mortels d'a present comme sur nos peres. C'est à les imiter que consiste la vraie sagesse.

SERVILIE

Eh bien, mon frere! Qu'avés-vous à repondre. [*Vous me paroissez un peu confondus.*]

CATON

Finissons tous ces verbiages.

BACCHIS

Voilà [*par ou l'on se sauve*] quand on n'a rien de bon à repondre.

CATON

En un mot je ne veux point contracter d'obligation avec personne. [*Je trouverai des esclaves plus obeissans pour*] [81.55] executer mes ordres. *Je vais les chercher.*

Scene 4ᵉ

Servilie, Bacchis

BACCHIS

Voilà un homme de bien mauvaise humeur!

SERVILIE

Tu le vois, tu l'entends, eh bien! j'ai beau le dire à tout le monde, personne ne le croit; et c'est précisement de son humeur [*bourue, et de*] son avarice qu'il [*usurpe*] cette reputation de vertu qui [*eblouit une partie des Romains car l'autre le connoit*].

BACCHIS

C'est votre frere, mais vous ne vous ressemblés guère.

SERVILIE

Je crains si fort de lui ressembler, qu'il n'est point d'extremité contraire que je ne saisisse.

BACCHIS

On le voit bien.

SERVILIE

Il m'est dejà venu dix fois dans l'esprit de faire jetter dans le Tibre tous les presents dont il fait tant de bruit pour lui faire voir mon désintéressement.

BACCHIS

Ah, ma chere maitresse! Attendés au moins que j'aie loué des plongeurs.

SERVILIE

Il n'y a que la main de Cesar qui me retient, c'est le seul motif qui me rend chers tous les dons qu'il m'a faits. Mais Bacchis, il ne vient point.

BACCHIS

Bon! madame, viendra-t'il?

SERVILIE

Que veux-tu donc dire?

[81.56]   BACCHIS

Cesar est si volage! Il n'a pas plutot obtenu une permission qu'il ne s'en soucie plus.

SERVILIE

Oh! Tes défiances m'impatientent. Ne veux-tu pas que Cesar arrive ici, quand il y voit mon frere? Je suis sure qu'il se sera caché quelque part dans le bois qui est au fond du jardin, ou il meurt de froid.

BACCHIS

Allons voir.

SERVILIE

Non, il faut que tu restes ici pour l'attendre. Au cas qu'il vienne de ce coté, il faut bien qu'il y trouve quelqu'un.

BACCHIS

C'est à dire que vous irés seule le chercher dans ce bois.

SERVILIE

Je m'en garderai bien. Je veux cependant savoir s'il y est.

BACCHIS

Comment ajuster tout cela?

SERVILIE

Je ne sais, c'est ce qui m'embarasse.

BACCHIS

Prenés une autre de vos femmes.

SERVILIE

Mais, Bacchis, ce seroit multiplier ma confidence malàpropos.

BACCHIS

Allés donc seule, vous en mourés d'impatience.

SERVILIE

Je vais seulement voir de loin si je l'apperçois, et je reviens ici dans l'instant.

[81.57]   Scene 5ᵉ

Bacchis, Cesar qui entre du coté opposé
à la sortie de Servilie

BACCHIS

Voilà une pauvre cervelle furieusement derangée . . . Bon! Voici justement ce qu'elle cherche. Seigneur, attendés ici un moment. Ma maitresse vous cherche, elle ne peut être loin, je vais l'avertir.

CESAR

Arrete, Bacchis, nous pourons aisément nous rencontrer. [x] J'ai un mot à te dire "en parti entier".

BACCHIS

Quoi! C'est-là l'impatience que vous temoignés aprés ce que vous avés ecrit ce matin!

CESAR

Bacchis, je te prie d'accepter ce collier.

BACCHIS

Ah! Ceci n'est plus si indifferent.

CESAR

Moi indifferent! Je n'eus jamais tant d'amour.

BACCHIS *à part*

Par Venus! Je commence à vous croire.

CESAR

Ah Bacchis! Si tu savois la situation de mon ame.

BACCHIS

Je vous avoue que je ne la croiois pas telle que je la vois. Je suis même fachée a present d'avoir tant contrarié ma maitresse.

CESAR

Bacchis, ou est Cornelie? Je meurs si je ne la vois un moment.

BACCHIS

Cornelie! La distraction est un peu forte. Servilie vous voulés dire?

[81.58]   CESAR

Crois-tu que ses rigueurs finissent?

169

BACCHIS

Eh mais! Ses rigueurs sont assés douces.

CESAR

Si tu savois comme elle m'a traité.

BACCHIS

Ou l'avés-vous vue?

CESAR

Ici, dans ce vestibule.

BACCHIS

Ouais! Pourquoi m'en a-t'elle fait mistere?

CESAR

Elle me hait, Bacchis; je suis bien malheureux!

BACCHIS

Je n'y comprends rien. Ou prenés-vous qu'elle vous haisse? J'aurois cru moi qu'elle vous aimoit plus que vous ne l'aimés.

CESAR

Helas! Puis-je seulement me flater de l'etre?

BACCHIS

Oh! Pour le coup je m'y perds. Jamais je n'aurois soupconné Cesar d'etre modeste ni défiant sur son merite.

CESAR

Ma chere Bacchis! Ne pourois-tu me procurer encore un moment d'entretien.

BACCHIS

Soiés donc d'accord avec vous même. Je voulois aller l'avertir, vous me retenés.

CESAR

Elle ne viendroit pas. Il faudroit par adresse . . .

BACCHIS

Je reponds que son impatience passe de beaucoup la vôtre.

CESAR

Ah! Tu ne connois pas la fille de Cinna.

[81.59]   Saturnales[4]

BACCHIS

Encore! Expliquons-nous, de qui parlés-vous? [x]

CESAR

De Cornelie. Est-il une autre femme qui puisse inspirer à Cesar un amour si violent?

BACCHIS

Ah ma pauvre maitresse! Je n'avois que trop bien deviné.

CESAR

Oui, Bacchis, tu vois la verité. Je ne voulois pas feindre avec toi, et tu ne voulois pas m'entendre. Puis-je esperer que tu voudras bien me servir?

BACCHIS

Tout le service que je puis vous rendre, c'est d'aller retrouver ma maitresse, et de l'empecher de vous voir. Je lui epargnerai un chagrin, et à vous un grand embarras.

CESAR

Eh quoi! Bacchis refuse de m'obliger.

[4] written in pencil at the top of the page, in an unknown hand, probably that of a cataloguer.

BACCHIS

Je ne puis vous obliger d'avantage. Adieu, seigneur, je suis votre servante.

Scene 6ᵉ ..

Cesar, Cratinus

CRATINUS

Ou donc vous êtes-vous fouré? J'ai parcouru toutes les recoins de la maison sans vous trouver.

CESAR

Et moi j'ai cherché vainement Cornelie. Elle s'est enfermée surement pour ne me [*ᵃ*plus revoir*ᵃ*].

[81.60]   **CRATINUS**

Je suis même sorti de la maison, croiant que vous l'aviés abandonné, et si je ne vous ai pas trouvé, du moins n'ai-je pas perdu tout à fait mes peines.

CESAR

Comment?

CRATINUS

J'ai rencontré un esclave de Cinna qui m'a dit que son maitre étoit arrivé.

CESAR

Ah Cratinus! Quel bonheur! Courons le chercher.

CRATINUS

Ne bougés. Il va venir ici dans un instant reprendre sa fille.

CESAR

Je l'attends, [*ᵃ*et je ne le quitte plus. Il faut qu'il*ᵃ*] cède à mon impatience, qu'il m'accorde sa fille, ou je ne sais à quelles extrémités je pourois me porter.

CRATINUS

Mais oserés-vous paroitre devant Cinna, ainsi travesti?

CESAR

Pourquoi pas? Cinna est un bon homme [*gaie, de bonne humeur*]. Rien ne le blesse de ce qui regarde l'amusement.

CRATINUS

A propos, j'oubliois un billet que j'ai à vous remettre.

CESAR

De qui? [x]

CRATINUS

De Servilie.

CESAR

Tu peux le garder.

[90.53]⁵   [*Scene 7ᵉ

Cesar, Cratinus, Caton

CATON

Quels sont ces esclaves etrangers. L'un d'eux lit un billet. Sachons ce que c'est. Il ne faut rien negliger. Que faites-vous ici? Que lisez-vous? Justes dieux! Me tromperois-je? Est-ce Cesar que je vois?

CESAR

Lui meme, et sans doute Caton ne s'atendois pas a le trouver ici.

⁵ the rest of the play (III.vii-ix) is entirely in mme de Graffigny's hand, and bound in a separate volume of the papers. The draft, presumably by Bret, from which she worked after this point, must have been discarded altogether, if indeed it ever existed.

173

CATON

C'est donc ainci que tu viens braver ma colere. Cesar chez Caton!
Quelle audace!

CESAR

Si Caton vouloit quitter ses preventions et s'il connoissoit bien le
cœur de Cesar

CATON

Je connois tes mauvaises intentions, cela me sufit pour te jurer une
haine eternelle.

CESAR

Et moi pour vous offrir l'amitié la plus sincere. Je vous rend justice,
Caton, plus que vous ne me la rendez. Vos intentions sont droite mais
vous partez d'un faux principe.

CATON

Ce n'est point ici le lieu de discuter nos raisons, c'est le senat ou je
te cite qui en jugera. Dis-moi quel est le sujet de cette mascarade ridicule. Quelle intrigue secrete t'a fait prendre un tel deguisement? Ai-je
quelqu'un dans ma maison qu'il te sois important de corrompre?
Quelle letre misterieuse lisois-tu là? Tout doit etre suspect de la part
de Cesar.

CESAR

Je ne le suis qu'a Caton. Il le dit a tous le monde et je ne m'en plains
qu'a lui. La simple curiosité de voir a quel point la joye est rependue
dans Rome m'a porté a parcourir les ruë. Je passois devant la porte de
Caton et j'ai voulu voir si sa depense en illumination egaloit ses
richesses.

[90.54]   CATON

Laissons, laissons ces vains discours. Cest ecrit que tu viens de
cacher ne peut manquer de m'etre suspect. O ma patrie! De combien
de piege secrets tu peux etre la proye.

CESAR

Caton aime mieux hazarder de se tromper que de manquer le plus leger pretexte de s'abbandonner a la defiance.

CATON

Ah, les artifices ne te manque pas. Avec tes froides railleries tu crois eluder les effets de ma vigilance. Mais tu m'aurois deja montré ce papier s'il ne justifioit pas mes soubsons.

CESAR

J'apercois Cinna; voulez-vous le prendre pour juge?

Scene 8ᵉ

Caton, Cesar, Cratinus, Cinna, Dromon

DROMON *a Cinna*

Seigneur, ne m'oubliez pas. Je suis perdu si je reste ici apres les Saturnales.

CINNA

Je te l'ai promis, compte sur ma parolle. Eh, bojour, mon viel ami. Coment va ta santé, celle de ta seur et celle de ma chere Cornelie? Mais que vois-je? Cesar chez Caton! En conversation familiere! J'en suis ravi, je vous le jure. J'aime l'union et je soufrois de votre injustice.

CATON

Soufrez donc encore car elle est plus alumée que jamais.

CINNA

Est-il vray, Cesar?

CESAR

Oui, segneur, du coté de Caton, car de la miene je n'eus jamais contre lui aucun ressentiment.

175

CINNA *a Caton*

Qu'as-tu a dire a cela. On ne sauroit parler plus honnetement.

CATON

Et agir avec plus de fourberie.

CINNA

Eh je ne suis jamais pour les invectives. J'ai remarqué qu'elles ne prouvent rien.

[90.55]   CATON

Eh bien, il faut donc metre les faits devant vos yeux. Obligez Cesar a vous montrer un ecrit qu'il lisoit quand je l'ai surpris ici dans l'equipage indessent ou vous le voiez.

CESAR

Il est vray, Cinna, que je suis honteux de paroitre a vos yeux sous ce deguisement.

CINNA

Eh, pourquoi? Les Saturnales l'autorise. Rien n'est si naturel que le plaisir a ton age. Et celui là est bien inocent.

CATON

Oui, s'il ne couvroit pas une trame odieuse contre la patrie.

CINNA

Si cela est, il a tort.

CATON

Quel sang froid! Il exciteroit seul ma colere quand je n'en aurois pas d'autres sujet.

CINNA

Fi, fi, ne parlons point de colere dans des jours consacrés a la joye. Je viens passer les Saturnales avec toi et je suis ravi que Cesar soit des notre.

CESAR

Caton ne me fait pas cet honneur. Le hazard seul m'a conduit chez lui.

CINNA *a Caton*

Cela est mal. Il faut oublier toutes rancune pour nous livrer a la joye.

CATON

Allez, de ce moment vous n'estes plus mon ami.

CINNA

Quoi, parce que je ne veux point epouser tes craintes, tes deffiances eternelles, tu me haïras? Ah notre ami, je te croiois plus sensé.

CATON

Pour savoir si j'ai tort, faites montrer a Cesar l'ecrit donc je vous parle.

[90.56]   CINNA (*a Cesar*)

Bon, allons, il faut le satisfaire. Est-il vrai d'abord que tu as un ecrit suspect?

CESAR

Oui, seigneur, mais il ne l'est que pour Caton.

CATON

Eh bien, en voulez-vous davantage?

CINNA

Cesar, des que tu conviens que les soubsons sont fondés, il faut les eclaircir.

CESAR

Je ne le puis.

177

CATON

Traitre, il faudra bien . . .

CESAR

Ne vous emportez pas. Jusqu'ici vous ne sauriez vous plaindre de ma moderation. Mais je ne pourois repondre qu'elle dura toujours.

CATON

Par combien d'artifice il veut se soustraire a ma penetration. Est-il un fourbe plus adroit?

CESAR

Je vous ai deja dit de vous moderer. Et si vous me poussez a bout toute la honte de mes pretendus artifices retombera sur vous.

CATON

Tous tes detours sont inutils. Il faut voir cet ecrit.

CESAR

Je vous avertis encore de ne point me presser.

CATON

Ah, treve de fourberies.

CESAR

Je n'y tiens plus, je prends Cinna a temoin que vous meritez ce qui va vous arriver. Tenez, Cinna, lisez.

CINNA

Volontier. Si cela pouvoit vous accorder, j'en serois fort aise. (*Il lit.*) Venez, charmant esclave. Que rien ne vous soit suspect. Mon frere est trop occupé du chagrin que lui cause la joye publique pour s'apercevoir de votre deguisement. Venez jurer votre constant amour a la tendre Servilie.

[90.57]

CINNA

Ah ah ah, par Mercure le tour est bon. Eh bien, notre ami, es-tu satisfait? Faut-il denoncer Cesar au senat? Ah ah ah.

CATON

Lache, vous aprouvez toutes les perfidies de ce traitre. Je vous jure la meme haine qu'a lui. O ma patrie, ma patrie. *Il sort.*

Scene 9^e

Cinna, Cesar, Cratinus, Dromon

CESAR

Seigneur, je tombe a vos genoux.

CINNA

Tu ne m'as point offencé. Je connois Servilie. C'est une folle. Tu ne l'aime pas surement.

CESAR

Non, seigneur, la seule Cornelie est digne de mon homage. Je ne puis douter de votre parolle; mais je doute de son cœur et c'est pour moi le tourment le plus cruel.

CINNA

Elle seroit bien dificile vraiment si tu ne lui plaisoit pas. Si j'etois femme, moi qui te parles, je ne trouverois rien de si aimable que Cesar.

Scene derniere

Cinna, Cesar, Cornelie, Sostrata, Dromon, Cratinus

CORNELIE

Ah mon pere, qu'est-il arrivé? Caton vient de m'apprendre votre retour avec une colere et des imprecations contre Cesar qui me font trembler pour la republique.

179

CINNA

Va, va, la republique n'a rien a demeler la dedans. Tu sauras l'aventure a loisir. Il est maintenant question d'autre chose.

CESAR

Oui, belle Cornelie, vous alez decider du destin de Cesar. Si vous voiez avec dedain les bontés de Cinna pour moi, je suis le plus malheureux des Romains.

[90.58]   CINNA

Bon, ne voila-t-il pas comme l'amour tourne la tete. Crois-tu, mon ami, qu'elle va te faire une declaration en ma presence? Ça la main. Je vous unis, et je crois, Cornelie, que tu ne te plaindras pas de la violence que je te fais.

CORNELIE

Mon pere . . .

CESAR

S'il dependoit de moi, madame, j'exigerois moins de votre obeissance.

CORNELIE

Je vous ai dit, Cesar, qu'elle etoit le premier et le plus cher de mes devoirs.

DROMON

Seigneur Cinna, songez a moi.

CINNA

Caton ne peut te refuser a la loi qui m'otorise a te prendre a mon servisse. Tu es a moi.

DROMON

Me voila en sureté. Soiez donc les temoins de mon savoir faire dans une illumination et un balet que j'ai preparé pour couronner le premier jour des Saturnales.

Le theatre s'illumine et on danse

Fin[a]]

BIBLIOGRAPHY

I

Manuscripts

Bret, Antoine. Draft of *Les Saturnales*. Bibliothèque nationale, Manuscrits, Nouvelles acquisitions françaises 9209, ff.311-316.

Graffigny, mme de. Graffigny papers (cited as GP). Beinecke Rare Book and Manuscript Library, Yale University. The Graffigny papers consist of seventy-eight volumes bound in boards; the volumes bear numbers from an old classification which went at least to 100; the pages were numbered in pencil sometime before 1965.

– Other papers concerning mme de Graffigny are to be found in the Bibliothèque nationale, Manuscrits, Nouvelles acquisitions françaises 15579-15581 and 15589-15592; and in private collections.

– *Les Saturnales*. Fair copy in an unknown hand. Oesterreichische Nationalbibliothek, ser. nov. 2694, no.220.

II

Printed sources

Besterman, Theodore, *Voltaire*, 3rd edition, Chicago 1976.

Bruwaert, Edmond, 'Madame de Graffigny et Jean-Jacques Rousseau', *Revue hebdomadaire* (1924), viii.567-592.

Clément, Pierre, and Joseph de La Porte, *Anecdotes dramatiques*. Paris 1775.

Collé, Charles, *Journal et mémoires*, ed. Honoré Bonhomme. Paris 1868.

Cokayne, G. E., *The Complete peerage*, revised by Vicary Gibbs. London 1949.

Courtois, Louis-J., 'Chronologie critique de la vie et des œuvres de Jean-Jacques Rousseau', *Annales Jean-Jacques Rousseau* (1923), xv.

Crocker, Lester G., *Jean-Jacques Rousseau: the quest (1712-1758)*. New York 1968.

Desnoiresterres, Gustave, *Voltaire et la société au XVIIIe siècle*. Paris 1871.

Dictionnaire de biographie française, ed. J. Balteau, et al. Paris 1933- .

Dictionnaire historique et biographique de la Suisse, ed. Victor Attinger, Marcel Godet and Henri Türler. Neuchâtel 1928.

Durey de Noinville, J. B., *Histoire du théâtre de l'Académie royale de musique en France*, 2e éd. Paris 1757; reprinted Genève 1972.

Epinay, madame d', *Histoire de madame de Montbrillant*, ed. Georges Roth. Paris 1951.

Etienne, Louis, 'Un roman socialiste d'autrefois', *Revue des deux mondes* (15 juillet 1871), xciv.454-464; reprinted in Nicoletti.

181

Graffigny, madame de, *Lettres d'une Péruvienne*, ed. Gianni Nicoletti. Bari 1967.

Guéhenno, Jean, *Jean-Jacques; en marge des Confessions*. Paris 1948.

Havens, George R., 'Voltaire's meeting with Rousseau', *Diderot studies* (forthcoming).

Helvétius, *Correspondance complète*, ed. David W. Smith et al. (forthcoming).

Helvétius, madame, *Correspondance complète*, ed. Peter Allan, unpublished thesis. University of Toronto 1976.

Iselin, Isaak, *Pariser Tagebuch 1752*, ed. Ferdinand Schwarz. Basel 1919.

Keys, A. C., *Antoine Bret, 1717-92: the career of an unsuccessful man of letters*. Auckland 1959.

Khevenhüller-Metsch, Fürsten Johann Josef, *Aus der Zeit Maria Theresias: Tagebuch 1742-1767*. Wien 1907-1917.

Lancaster, Henry C., *French tragedy in the time of Voltaire*, Baltimore 1950.

La Porte, Joseph de, *L'Observateur littéraire*. Amsterdam and Paris 1758.

Launay, Denise, ed., *La Querelle des Bouffons*. Genève 1973.

Le Clerc, Paul O., *Voltaire and Crébillon père: history of an enmity*. Studies on Voltaire, cxv: 1973.

Maugras, Gaston, *Querelles de philosophes: Voltaire et Jean-Jacques Rousseau*. Paris 1886.

May, Georges, *Rousseau par lui-même*. Paris 1961.

Mercure de France. Paris 1749-1758.

Nicoletti *see* Graffigny, *Lettres d'une Péruvienne*.

Noël, Georges, *Une 'primitive' oubliée de l'école des 'cœurs sensibles' : madame de Grafigny*. Paris 1913.

Pichois, Claude and René Pintard, *Jean-Jacques entre Socrate et Caton*. Paris 1972.

Prévost, Antoine-François, translator's preface to Samuel Richardson, *Lettres angloises, ou histoire de miss Clarisse Harlowe*. Londres 1751.

Ritter, Eugène, 'Les premières relations entre Voltaire et Rousseau', *Annales Jean-Jacques Rousseau* (1916-1917), xi.

Rousseau, Jean-Jacques, *Correspondance complète*, ed. R. A. Leigh. Oxford 1965- (cited as Leigh).

Rousseau, Jean-Jacques, *Lettre à M. d'Alembert sur les spectacles*, in *Œuvres complètes*. Paris 1852, iii.

Rousseau, Jean-Jacques, *Œuvres complètes*, ed. Bernard Gagnebin and Marcel Raymond, 'Bibliothèque de la Pléiade'. Paris 1959- ; vol.i: *Confessions et autres œuvres autobiographiques*, 1964 (original edition 1959); vol. ii: *La Nouvelle Héloïse, théâtre, poésie, essais littéraires*, 1964; vol.iii: *Du contrat social, écrits politiques*, 1964; vol.iv: *Emile, éducation, morale, botanique*, 1969; (cited as *Œuvres*).

Showalter, English, 'The beginnings of madame de Graffigny's literary career', in *Essays on the age of the Enlightenment in honor of Ira O. Wade*, ed. Jean Macary. Paris 1977, pp.293-304.

Showalter, English, 'Madame de Graffigny and her salon', in *Studies in eighteenth-century culture*, ed. Ronald C. Rosbottom. Madison 1977, vi.377-391.

Showalter, English, 'Sensibility at Cirey: mme Du Châtelet, mme de Graffigny, and the *Voltairomanie*', *Studies on Voltaire* (1975), cxxxv. 181-192.

Showalter, English, *Voltaire et ses amis d'après la correspondance de mme de Graffigny*. Studies on Voltaire, cxxxix: 1975.

Sotheby and Co, *Bibliotheca Phillippica*: sale catalogue of 28 June 1965, pp.43-60, lots 114-132.

Starobinski, Jean, *Jean-Jacques Rousseau: la transparence et l'obstacle.* Paris 1957.

Studies on Voltaire and the Eighteenth Century, founded by Theodore Besterman, edited by Haydn T. Mason. Oxford 1955- .

Turgot, Anne-Robert-Jacques, *Lettre à madame de Graffigny sur les Lettres Péruviennes* (1751), in *Œuvres,* ed. Eugène Daire. Paris 1844, vol. ii; reprinted in Nicoletti.

Voltaire, *Correspondance and related documents,* ed. Theodore Besterman (cited as Best.D), in *The Complete works.* Oxford 1968-, vols. 85-135 (1968-1977).

INDEX OF PROPER NAMES